Walk to Freedom

+

The Book of the Highest Good: Volume Two

By

Joyce McCartney

For Peace and Light Association

Produced by Positive Options, Inc.

ISBN: 978-0-9897088-0-7

Copyright: July 31, 2013 by Joyce McCartney

All rights reserved. No part of this book may be reproduced or transmitted in any form or by any means, electronic or mechanical, including photocopying, recording, or by any information storage or retrieval system, without written permission from the author, except inclusion of brief quotations in a review. Contact: peaceandlight01@aol.com

Legal Disclaimer: All characters and people in this book and all books in the series should be considered fictional. No harm is intended or made to any person living or historical or any system of beliefs. The opinions of non-physical beings recorded here are their own and should not be considered as those of the author, producer or any associates.

Cover Design by Adam Brown

First Edition, 2013

Table of Contents

Preface 1

Introduction 4

    The Long Story 5

Chapter One: Adieu and Godspeed 19

    Message from the Peaceful One 20

    The Dialogue 20

    The Reading: One Mind, One Thought,
    One Being. 31

    Commentary 33

Chapter Two: One Step At a Time 35

Chapter Three: Help of a Higher Kind 46

Chapter Four: The Travelers 54

    Early Spring Trip 55

    Commentary 70

    Dialogue, Later in the Spring 72

    Early Summer Trip 87

    A Reading from The Great Oneness 89

Chapter Five: The Runaways 112

    Commentary 117

Chapter Six: The Soul's Progress 119

    A Reading..120

    A Reading..128

Chapter Seven: Trusting the Highest Good 135

The End of Volume Two..161

Forward to Volume Three 162

Resources 165

    Recommended Websites.......................................165

Preface

This is a preface to peace. The peace that surpasses understanding is the type of peace that cannot be taken seriously by a Conscious Mind. Rather one must rise higher and enter into the realm of the Higher Mind to survive. Thus, it can be said that no one who enters here can understand what is given unless they enter with their Higher Mind and are at rest with their fearful Conscious Mind.

Therefore, it is advisable to make the acquaintance of the two minds by reading the first Volume: **The Book of the Highest Good: A Beginning Experience** and make the final decision as to which mind is about to be engaged. If the Conscious Mind is chosen, there is no point to reading this book. In fact, it will be so distasteful as to have to put it aside in favor of much more compelling mistruths or even half truths. However, if the Higher Mind is chosen, then there is much to be said and in the end there will never be another one of any mind that can be sad or left in misery.

With this said, there is yet another decision to be made. With what mind would you have me write this volume? If it is written with a Conscious Mind, however kind, it will seem profound but yet mistaken. Surely it is a confusion of the mind of the author. However, with the intention changed to that of the Higher Mind, there is a distinct lesson to be learned. If your Higher Mind and our Higher Mind are in sync, then it will be an incomparable conversation. For that reason, the pronoun "we" or "our" will be used to refer to the Oneness of Higher Mind which is speaking.

For a departure is indeed taking place. It is a departure from a territory of grief and a world of misery to be left behind to vanish all of the sudden for lack of participation. It would be followed by an arrival to a world of peace, health, sage guidance and higher understanding than the Conscious Mind could ever achieve. This would be much like one who takes the strong medicine and swallows it hard and then awaits much relief later. The readers of the first Volume have taken the first swallow and, in allowing the thoughts of the previous book to have entered into their minds and to give them some nourishment, have experienced what is tantamount to letting the Titanic crash into a great iceberg only to find that it did not sink after all.

And so we will remind the reader that is used to being so loved by the author as to have been addressed as Beloved One, to be reminded to find relief not just with one more line or chapter, but to find it as a deep well of life within oneself where it will grow forever.

Thus we will begin with the first lines of a wise poem we composed just for this occasion:

Faith Unnecessary

How well does it rain
when the sun remains on retainer?

How well does it rain
in a heart when grief can be washed away?

Have you not spent many a day
living with rain, missing the sun?

Fear not; wish not, for the sun is a shining
no matter the rain.

We attend your every breath and
command the rain and clouds.

Come talk with us and find your peace.

Introduction

With this mysterious warning as a preface, the reader dare not enter without some instruction. Once one has read The Long Story and truly understood its content, one cannot ever again consider oneself to be bad, ugly or even uncivil, only fearful. Therefore, accepting the proposition that all humans are at once Beings of Light and at the same time fearful little minds in distress, we undertake the explanation of many a situation to guide the way from syndromes of fear to expanding happiness.

And with that as our purpose, there is ever the cure of an insightful question and answer. So therefore, the dialogues will continue with many a story of grief relived and happiness restored. And in the end, there will only be one story and only one thought. For we would all be one if only it were understood from whence all existence comes.

We begin at the beginning once again by including The Long Story at the onset. After a thorough reading, it will be set aside and many characterizations of both misery and peace will be discussed both from the standpoint of suffering as well as the healing, so that all who have been helped can become helpers. As it arose from the experience of one who sat at a computer as a small one of peace who called herself to task for the settling of all debts and the righting of all woes and wished it the same for all others, it is she who wishes to read it to you herself. Why not read it with your heart wide open?

The Long Story

This is a very long story that I am about to tell you, and it is essentially a love story.

So settle in for a view of how love created a world of peace.

In the beginning, as it says in the Bible, there was God. And God loved being the great thought of love and the Source of all life. There was God and nothing else. Everything was in peace.

In one great moment, God wanted to love someone else, and so created many souls in a great act of conception. This is who we are. We are those souls. We were created from the substance of God to BE LOVED and to be companions in the giving and receiving of love. We were created out of the substance of love, for that is all that there was or is. Love is our nature, the same as our Creator.

Later, God wanted us to be able to love back as beings of thought and action, and so a universe of places to experience life and love was created in a big bang. The stars, solar systems, and galaxies appeared. We entered in spirit form into these places where we experienced many things, sharing them with God, always coming back to the appreciation of how much we were loved.

We loved giving love back to God and to each other and created many beautiful experiences including procreation. At all times while we were in physical existence, we existed in spirit form as well and enjoyed The Presence of God, which was very peaceful, blissful and safe.

Being in the peaceful Presence of God is our Highest Good. In fact, we have to be peaceful to get there and stay there. If fear creeps in, the Higher Mind vanishes and the Conscious Mind takes over once again.

In spirit form, there is no separation among the many souls. We are always in total and constant communication with each other and know every thought and experience that any of us have. We also know the Mind of God, for we are of the same mind. Being with God and each other is our only desire. This is the Greatest Good that we can ever have.

In this spirit form, we are known as the Great Oneness. And we live as ever-changing orbs of light in peace and security, having no fear.

When we came to the earth, we found animals and plants and became interested in the experience of living in a physical body. The DNA of the hominid form was developed as the best vehicle to house the great mind of our high souls. We wanted to be creators like God who gave us life, so we created a smaller version of our great Soul Mind and experienced living within this small, undeveloped mind, essentially a baby mind living in the human body. We refer to it as Conscious Mind and with it we fully experience physical life. The Soul or Higher Mind, being in spirit form, experiences everything at once, but the Conscious Mind can only know and experience things one at a time because it lives in time and space.

The Conscious Mind is a very limited version of Soul Mind but is of the same construction and ancestry. It desires to be loved and to know truth, however, living in time, it learns in steps and does not always use its free will wisely because it does not know the whole truth at once. These Conscious Minds needed to learn to deal with the Higher Mind through cooperation, much like a teenager learning to drive a car. After each lifetime, the individual Conscious Mind was brought back to the soul. The life experiences were reviewed so a decision could be made about having another lifetime to increase the cooperation between the two minds – and thus achieve the destiny of the Conscious Mind to "grow up" and be in complete cooperation with Higher Mind. When this is achieved, both enjoy the Presence of God as wise and loving souls.

Thus, human kind developed with two minds, the Higher Mind of the Soul and the limited mind of the Human Conscious Mind. It was a very confusing experience because the two minds were quite different.

The Higher Mind channeled only the love of God, but the Conscious Mind did not see the whole picture and thought that we were all separate. It could not recall who it was, why it was here and where it was going. It did not remember the Presence of God except as a distant yearning, so it often chose fear, anxiety, depression, conflict, greed and aggression as a way of life.

These experiences of fear proliferated as more and more humans populated the earth and the belief in fear and separation became part of all human experience. As societies developed, some discovered the fact of the two minds and were able to access both. Others emphasized only the Conscious Mind and participated in war, greed and cruelty, thereby creating poverty, disease and vast amounts of human suffering.

These fears became a way of life, as one civilization followed another – some better, some worse. Thus, human history was fashioned from these two minds at work on the earth.

It was mainly the great spiritual teachers who talked about the Higher Mind and its trademark feeling: Peace.

They led the way to a better understanding of the human condition. They taught how to access the Higher Mind for that precious guidance of how to be safe and peaceful.

Peace is so clearly a characteristic of the Higher Mind that it is the password needed to enter it, and the lack of it is a sure sign that we have left the Higher Mind and are now operating in fear, which arises from the Conscious Mind.

Thus, we come to the love story of you and your soul. You are one of those souls, a great Being of Light, living in a physical body with a Conscious Mind, possibly confused about the experience of the two Minds. You seek the faint and happy memory of the Presence of God available in the Higher Mind, but see the evidence of fear all around you in the structures of civilization and doubt its existence. Sometimes you feel the peace and love, and sometimes you don't. You want to have that peace all of the time but don't know how to achieve it. So you become a hesitant seeker of your first Lover, God.

Fortunately, we have the great teachers to guide us. One of these was Edgar Cayce, who, in deep sleeping trance, spoke from his Higher Mind and gave beautiful, healing readings. All of this evidence of the benign reality of the Higher Mind was to help us to understand and use the access to the Higher Mind, bring the Conscious Mind to wisdom, and to find our way back to God's Presence. The information from the Higher Mind is always directed to the Highest Good of all beings, meaning the Presence of God.

Cayce demonstrated that Higher Mind can retell the history of the earth, give technical solutions to modern problems, suggest healing remedies, give great guidance for a better life and much more. Wouldn't you like to be in that peace and love of the Higher Mind more often? Wouldn't you want the unique wisdom of your own soul guiding you through your daily life experiences, unerringly taking you back to the loving Presence of God? Wouldn't you like to be free of fear, depression, anger and grief?

There is a very clear method for moving between the Conscious Mind and the Higher Mind, and we will teach you that method now. When you are finished, you will have one small message from your own Higher Mind guiding you back to the Presence of God in small daily steps. It will involve bringing your Conscious Mind into cooperation and finding that the Higher Mind does indeed lead the Conscious Mind to a much better life. Thus you can lose all sense of doubt and fear. If you ask for a daily message from Higher Mind with the Intention for the Highest Good, it will bring you back to happiness, which by necessity would include better health, fortune, prosperity, social life and relationships.

These messages are from your soul, in cooperation with all of the other souls who are in constant communication with each other. They assist anyone who asks by responding from the great stores of information on everything that has ever been experienced by them. You can communicate with any soul that you wish, including those who have passed over, just by asking.

You can receive guidance on many problems and projects, even highly technical ones. The Great Oneness has a sense of humor and a gentle loving way of helping and teaching us. They are the network of mind, the fabric of space and time, and they would love to help you because you are one of them, a part of the Great Oneness.

Here's how it works. First you must be peaceful, because that is how the Higher Plane works. The minute you are in doubt, fear or conflict, you revert back to the Conscious Mind, so we will do a short relaxation exercise and use some imagery to get you peacefully started. The next thing is to set the Intention for the Highest Good and nothing else. After all, you wouldn't want anything else for yourself or anyone else.

Finally, see yourself as one who is loved, waiting for someone who loves you, to communicate with you. This one who loves you is content that all is good and that nothing of harm can come to anyone including you. Then you can ask away. Begin a journal for your notes, and all that is for your Highest Good will be given to you and nothing else.

Keep in mind that it is never in your Highest Good to be frightened, criticized, judged, or sacrificed for anyone or anything else. You are to be treated with nothing but love. There is no guilt, judgment or punishment, no matter what you have done, only loving help. Such fearful and negative thoughts can reside only in the Conscious Mind and will not manifest unless you chose them with intensity. Since you are not going to be listening to them for a while, you are in for a nice experience. Go ahead and give it a try.

Relaxation exercise: Sit as comfortably as you can and take three long, deep breaths, each slower than the one before. Imagine yourself floating on a soft cloud with warm sun and fresh breezes, and just rest and listen. The cloud supports you in perfect comfort and security. Then let the Intention for the Highest Good come from your heart and see it bloom like a flower all around you. It is soft, but very strong. As you look around, you notice others floating on their clouds. One especially nice cloud comes close to you and a hand reaches out to you. You reach out to touch the hand and suddenly you know that you have found your Higher Mind. Once you are there, let questions come to mind and listen for an answer, accepting whatever you get, a feeling, a song, an image, a word or anything at all.

Ask another question and wait for an answer. Do this over and over again until the process gets clearer and easier to do. Keep notes in your journal and see the progress. The most important question will always be: What is my Highest Good today?

Remember to refrain from judging what you get or doubting yourself or your readings. Just do it again and again. It will get better and better.

Test your readings with these questions: Does the giver of this message know me very well? Does the giver of this message love me very well? Is this message free from any fear or doubt? If you get a "no" on any of these questions, you are not fully in the Higher Mind. If you get anything fearful or judgmental, ask to be given true loving help. Keep trying until you get a "yes" to these questions all of the time.

And now we will let you rest on that peaceful cloud and listen to the guidance of your own Higher Mind. Take three long, slow deep breaths, rest on your cloud and listen to someone who loves you.

Chapter One: Adieu and Godspeed

Once again, I am sitting alone in my sunny window on my small farm in rural Ohio. This time, I'm watching my two content riding mules graze in the pasture. It has snowed for several days, and the ground is very muddy but, of course, today the sun is shinning. I am now thinking of my five-year journey that started with the first sunny window experience. I remember how I started out with such self-judgment and doubt, wondering what I had done so wrong as to deserve the second divorce of my life. As I struggled to understand, I found myself talking to both of my two minds, the Fearful One (the Conscious Mind) and the Peaceful One (the Higher Mind of the Soul). And so as my two minds were discussing my fate, I began my journey, traveling through fears, doubt, and grief and finally arriving at a new understanding that indeed all was good from the start and would continue to be so or, at least, that was what the Peaceful One said.

I had come to so enjoy and depend on the daily dialogues with the Peaceful One, that I found it to be the model of what a good relationship should be like. But with the grief behind, was I completely happy? Not quite. There was still much to be learned. Would you, the reader accompany me once more to see where this trail will lead? You know by now that it will be only good.

+

Message from the Peaceful One

With this one saying goodbye to grief, where would one go on a long journey, if not to a better place? Therefore, we have in store for the reader, a longing goodbye to the grief presented in the first volume and a bon voyage party of peace to which all are invited, if they would care to bring themselves as they are and to change their garments from the drab to the glamorous. For once one is attired with the same brilliance as one IS, then all that was foretold will be as promised. Indeed it will be far beyond the expectation of a small mind to conceive. Therefore, we find the narrator once again installed in her sunny window at peace with herself at last, but still searching for the tools of the trade to make the mighty ship truly unsinkable.

The Dialogue

Joyce: I've never been one to complain when I am in your company, but sometimes I feel happy and complete and then sometimes I don't. I know the direction that I want to go, but it is so confusing. In addition, I keep circling around one central issue the gives me great pain from time to time. Can we talk?

Peaceful One: Upon the diet of potato chips there is the constant need to be pleased with the crunch and the taste. But after eating just one, there is the need to eat just one more to experience once more that happiness of the first taste. Then one has more and more, but is never satisfied more than once. Is that what you want to talk about?

Joyce: Good, you made me laugh. Yes, when I have a good experience and feel happy, it leaves me hungry for more and sure enough I look for it in the same places but it's different each time.

Peaceful One: If one experience of happiness leads one to find even more, wouldn't that be a grand plan for the perfection of one who needs to be completely happy and always able to find more without one ounce or instant of pain?

Joyce: So you are saying that there is good in this syndrome. That while we try to find happiness after it is missed, we confront yet another painful fear or ask for more to satisfy us and take off yet another layer of grief?

Peaceful One: Every time that you are unhappy is a moment of truth not to be missed. For how precise is it to just wander along the path to enlightenment when you could have a sense of direction? In fact, each time you choose to be happy, you strengthen your resolve and find happiness more easily. How good a plan is that?

Joyce: So it's like erasing thoughts and choices that mar a day of happiness, so to speak. We see happiness more and get better and better at eliminating or preventing disastrous thought. Sort of like a continuous quality improvement at a manufacturing company. As soon as one defect is fixed a new one shows up for attention, but in the end so much is eliminated that the parts are of very high quality with very little effort.

Peaceful One: How sweet it is to be in contact with you. You have a knack of finding the truth wherever it is hiding and eliminating all lies and half-truths. Now which event has caused you pain recently and we will help you to repair it.

Joyce: I'm embarrassed to say that I still look at a relationship coming into my life as both a great pleasure to anticipate, but also a possible disaster. On the one hand, I expect another to bring me pleasure and happiness when I am sad, like the potato chip you talked about. On the other hand, I doubt that the love between us will be true and I fear that one of us will fail at living in the Highest Good and it will all turn out badly. I move from one thought to the other in misery.

Peaceful One: OK, let's take you by the one hand that counts, the upper hand. By meaningful glances of strength, there are some who have come to help you and have left a positive mark on your life, no harm and much good. Is that not so?

Joyce: Most certainly. These are my family and friends.

Peaceful One: Then let us come to some understanding of how this is happening because some of them are very free of fear and some are not so much, but each in their own way has made much progress toward peace while interacting with you.

Joyce: Yes, I recognize that. The Highest Good works beautifully in all who are in relationship with me, blessing both them and me. They are all perfect in that they are themselves in motion toward a good goal.

Peaceful One: Good, you mentioned the goal. For the intention is everything and the goal of any activity has all of the characteristics of a good goal or a poor one. For instance, let's look at a small child who wishes a cookie from the cupboard without the permission of her parents. She sets about bringing a stepstool, putting it in place, and then climbing up, opening the cupboard doors and helping herself while no one is looking. She has even learned not be found out so she is not scolded and denied her goal.

Joyce: How clever is that?

Peaceful One: But what is the goal and how is it blessed? Should it be seen that to eat a cookie is a delightful thing, and then it is a strong goal and needs strong action. If it is to be seen that eating cookies is bad for the health, particularly when one is a small child, then the action and results are not blessed with good. Which thought is resident in the mind of the perpetrator is the one that is important. So which one does she use, do you think?

Joyce: She has no idea of unhealthy eating habits. She has a good intention and does it safely and effectively.

Peaceful One: Then the parents have the unhealthy eating habits firmly implanted in their minds and nothing good will come of it. If they feel so, then the cookies should not be purchased and brought to the house. Only snacks of great good would be available and a small child could search for and snatch as long as she wishes.

Joyce: So what is the lesson for me? I got lost imagining her climbing the stepladder and finding fresh carrots in the cookie cupboard.

Peaceful One: Just so. Since one carrot equals two cookies in value, let's lay carrot cookies all around for one to find and devour at will. This is what the Great

Creator of the universe did so long ago. Unless you fear something is bad, it never really is.

Joyce: OK. Let me think about that. So where do our fears come from?

Peaceful One: Where else but from the fund of all things good viewed as bad, the Conscious Mind?

Joyce: There it is again! It is a repository of so many things that I find are barriers to my happiness. Do I have to clean it up or just stay out of it all together?

Peaceful One: One ounce of prevention is worth a pound of cure, so to speak, so let's take one step at a time. Would not the time travel machine of just one more reading about the time of Christ be of interest to you?

Joyce: Oh, I'd love that. I've long suspicioned that the New Testament accounts of Christ's life are just a tiny part of what it was really like. I always want to hear more. Go ahead, tell me the story.

Peaceful One: Well, then, we must recall that the lepers of the day were outcasts for a fine reason. They were left alone so as not to infect the rest of the population. Both they and their separated families were in agreement about this. So there was no harm except that they lived outside of the community and often got no clean water or good food. Christ wished to address this in one of his sermons. While sitting on a low hill, he told of the one aspect of life that made all situations to be livable and even joyful. He talked about the farmer in the field, sending his seeds into the wind to be carried across the field so they fall into the fertilized dirt, and spring to life. He compared this farmer to His Heavenly

Father who sent all souls into a physical universe with the intention for peace in all experiences.

In essence, the Heavenly Father gave his children a safe place in which to play and be assured that they never would be hurt or made to be less than they were in any way. With this in mind, it was his opinion that the lepers should be kindly treated even if they lived apart. Christ insisted that the helpers could lay their hands upon them and not retreat in fear for neither were they filthy nor were they harmful as far communication of the disease. He did so himself to show that he was never afraid to be among them. He helped them to heal themselves by showing them grace. For it is in grace that one is made to exist and it is in grace that one lives. So strong was his logic that none who came to help encountered harm and indeed found many a friend among them. Many of the lepers were invited back into their family homes with no ill regard or negative consequence.

We find that it is with so with many of the strong aspects of life. Should one be founded upon the conviction that one's life is whole and good even if you live as a leper, then thus it is: If not, then not.

Joyce: I love this story and I'm imagining the reunions of families with those who had been sent away. In fact, being a leper is the proverbial rejection of society personified. To think that it is unnecessary and reversible is pure Highest Good. But one great question comes to mind. If one thinks that something is bad and it is, which mind are you referring to? The Conscious Mind or the Higher Mind?

Peaceful One: Of which mind are you so sure that you can obtain this reading of grace if not the mind incapable of doubt? If so, then it is a good and valid reading, if not then not. This is the dynamic of doubt. In which mind does doubt reside?

Joyce: Only the Conscious Mind because the Higher Mind knows only of good and does not have to believe or doubt. It is at rest and content.

Peaceful One: Then you have found the source of not only the profound misery to which you referred, but also the profound grace. All in all a good line of questioning. To which mind do you attribute the art of questioning?

Joyce: The Conscious Mind, of course, because the Higher Mind never asks a question, for it knows all that there is to know.

So, let me take stock of this for a minute. Is the Conscious Mind a container of both love and doubt or a gatekeeper to either mind? The Conscious Mind does have free will.

Peaceful One: Both, for one mind is the better answerer, one mind at once living in time and space and the other at the same time living in eternity. For both experiences to coincide within the one existence, they must both be tied to the one personality that you would call "Me." If one wishes to turn to grief or to peace, it only requires the will to do so.

So a free will being is a grace to behold when happy and a disgrace when unhappy. Therefore, there is a race to see which will be the winner of the Puppy of the Month award and be selected to be given a better home than the shelter. If the puppy puddles too much and chews on the furniture, then it will be returned, but if it lifts the spirits of the children and guards the house, then it will be given high regard. One judged to be good and the other not good enough to keep.

Therefore, your comment as to which to endorse is essentially a ridiculous one. How could one endorse oneself one time and not another? Me is me and we are all one and the same. The shame of it all is the choice to be mean verses the choice to be good. To be mean, one says good is good for one being and bad is for the other. But for the rest of the time, no judgment at all is made, only a playful puppy making a mess in defense of his right to be growing up. If you need a timeout from playing with playful puppies, just step out for some fresh air in a nature retreat.

Joyce: So we are to love everyone even though they might make a mean decision. No one is good or bad, just children of God like the messy puppy experiencing life and slowly turning to the good. Is that what Christ meant to teach?

Peaceful One: Why don't you ask Him yourself? He just happens to be here in the studio asking about your progress. I'll put him on the speakerphone if you like.

Joyce: Please do. (With a smile)

Christ Consciousness: You watch and wait for your happiness like a mirrored lake waiting for the sun to rise so as to reflect its brilliance. Such is not the case. When I referred to My Heavenly Father, I meant to teach that there is a great brilliance in this world which is the Source of all existence without end, which leads us to the conclusion that we are sparks from the giant conflagration that is God.

Without Beings of Light to guide the way, there is no better way to deduce this than to see the sun rise each day and whether it is judged to be a good day or a bad day makes no difference. With this Divine wisdom, your days are all good days and no bad days exist unless you let your mind choose for it to be so.

Cease and desist from allowing others to be makers of your mind. Let none but the Divine be your partner of escape from the pain of the human enterprise. For I came to grant understanding as to the nature of all humankind to be equal and at peace and there is no other teaching that is so great.

Peaceful One: Let us proceed with the teaching of so subtle a thing as the nature of a spider web to be woven so as to catch a fly or float as a ribbon of peace in the air never to return again except as a puff of smoke. Did not the Father make all of these to be of Himself and thus he was a Maker of Makers. If your desire is to be happy, then it will be so. You are the creator of your happiness within the playground of happiness within which you were placed. If not, then not. It is just that simple and yet that complex.

Joyce: So I need to stop making judgments of any kind and to always choose happiness and everything will be fine, right?

Peaceful One: Was that not the subject of the first book? Did you not stop casting yourself as a victim when you found yourself to have a good purpose? Did you not proceed down a restful and benign path on which there was no harm and much good?

Joyce: Yes.

Peaceful One: Then you engineered your own demise as well as the remise. Congratulations, you have rendered yourself a willing vagrant of the Conscious Mind habit of self-discrimination. Just approve of yourself by making the choice to do so and all will be made to approve, no less, nor no more. To be content, however, to have no judgment is the better way. Without any judgment, there is the option to never be separate by being good or bad or better or worse, just be what one is.

Joyce: I get it. It was my habit of making judgments that lead me to the conclusion that there was a Fearful One and a Peaceful One. Actually, there is only one being worming its way through time and space, seeking experiences and being guided to return to the timeless experience of its parent.

Peaceful One: And so it is that this dialogue has come to an end. For how can we converse if we are not separate, but one. Should we but think with one thought?

Joyce: That sounds logical, but I don't know if I am quite there yet.

Peaceful One: Well, then, let's continue a while longer and even add a layer or two of additional personalities as we go along, for they are much like us and are in fact, much more than brothers and sisters. Merely mention their names and they will respond because they are thinking the same things as we are. No more or no less.

Joyce: Why do you keep saying: No more or no less?

Peaceful One: Because you keep insisting that I do. If not one, then two, if not less than one more. Just keep coming along with this line of thought and much more will be added, that, when all is added up, will make a whole if you want to think of it that way.

Joyce: OK, I get the point. Separation is a large part of our language and thinking and it will take me a while to adjust to a more unified way of being.

Peaceful One: Good, then let's have another one for the road and be on our way to yet another chapter for we have said goodbye to the concept of the Conscious Mind being a bad guy and need to say adieu to all of the grief that it brings. So as the song goes: "Goodbye, Farewell, Goodnight" in favor of singing "All for one and one for all."

Joyce: Thanks, I feel happy. Once again you have comforted me, taught me the truth and healed my two minds so that they can be one. Sweet!

The Reading:
One Mind, One Thought, One Being.

Peace and Light Association
Peaceandlight01@aol.com
PeaceandLight.net   Copyright: 2013

At this juncture, there is no mind to consider. In fact, the idea of a mind is quite likely to fall aside, having had too much wear and tear. In actuality, there is only a being of grace within which one must live and be and have experiences. If one would visualize a giant jelly-like organism, that would be a better concept of God than a person who is far distant. Once one has been spawned within the confines of the organism, one must live there and share all that is available, and, since the Great One is of great peace, there is only peace to be had. Therefore, let us all rejoice for we are all one in the same organism and never shall we leave. For in grace were we spawned, in grace do we live and in grace do we create. With this said there is nothing else to consider than that the thinking of the Great One is also the thinking of the little ones, for there isn't anything else to do or to be.

As to the aspect of one mind to be mean and the other graceful, there is no mean to be had. Once one has made the decision to be mean, then the meanness is entirely contained with oneself for it is really only a view or a belief that is projected for the play on words such as "Hey, meanie, I'm meaner than you. See if you can hit me. Bet you can't."

Thus when one wants to be mean, there are responses that their companions need to consider. First, the one deciding to be mean is doing harm only to him or herself and it means no more than that. Should they be made to be mean in the judgment of others, then much is lost for all have made the one to be mean and thus it takes on a life of its own and all can be made to be harmed and mean. All of history can be traced to the original intention to be mean. Should this ever be portrayed as an actor's proposal to portray a murder on the stage for the relief of the crowd to see the victim jump up unharmed at the end to accept the applause, then the deed has been portrayed correctly.

If one determines to never let anyone spoil their play with meanness and merely sends them away for a time-out until they come to their senses, then there is no reason for anger, grief, regret, revenge or even the thrill of victory. With that said, there is no good like grief relief of the self-kind. Should one determine to never cause oneself any reason for grief, then it will be so, and if some form of grief arises, the remedy would be to send the villain away and watch the victim get up, dust himself off and return to the cast to play yet another day. But if one would like to brush this all under the rug and play a new play, then they would join with the Reunioners who wish to portray the light of a new world of peace consciousness in which all who play are allowed to be free of the will to be mean.

With this we have come once again to the portrayal of all things to be green and, if not green, at least not purple with grief. And so it was given that those who have returned to find the world a mess of conceptions of harm and grief have arisen once again to take the lessons taught by Christ to the max and yes, this time the Titanic does not sink. It just floats away in peace.

Commentary

   Welcome Dear Reader to my private world. Not too many have been given access to it. You are welcome because you have decided to be happy as I have and want to learn how to do that so well that only happiness happens. But what of those who have not made such a decision? Do you have some of them in your life? Do they make you miserable as well as themselves?

   Being mindful that our mutual desire is to be happy and to have all beings happy, perhaps we need to revise our strategy. At first I thought, as you may have done, that the demise of the Conscious Mind was the way to go. Now it has been made clear, that only the choice to be mean is at fault. Or is it so? For if some intended to be mean, but found that everyone ignored them and sent them to their room, then they would have every opportunity to repair their thinking and return in a better frame of mind.

   I suppose that it is a form of forgiveness. So we have a responsibility to handle the meanies in the proper way. But most of all, dear loved one, do not ever take the fear projected by a meanie to be your own reality. It simply is not true, whatever it is. There is no reason under heaven or earth that you should ever be considered anything less that a happy Being of Light making your way through well chosen experiences, even that of being a leper. Refer the meanie to their own Higher Mind for better guidance or give them a time-out from interacting with you. While they are in time-out look eagerly for them to return in a good frame of mind for that is a vast pleasure not to be missed. It would comfort me to know that you will promise to do this. I want us all to know at all times that we are Beloved Ones and even if we are in time-out, that we are welcome to come back. With that settled, we can continue. Thank you. That feels so good to me.

Chapter Two: One Step At a Time

Joyce: What is the topic for today?

Peaceful One: That depends on your needs for today. Let's say that your need is to listen to yet another form of history full of war, rage, despair, hunger for love, etc. Then we would alert you to yet another time in history to explore and give you spectacular readings on that. Another typical need of yours is to begin a new book and so we would do so, filling your every need. Yet there is another type of neediness for you to consider. What if the need for the day is contentment?

Joyce: OK, I'll go for that. Let's say that I just want to be content and enjoy everything. But what about those that I meet who are in such pain and I want to help them?

Peaceful One: For certain, be sure that once that the trail to happiness over the rainbow has been opened, that many will come and trod the same path noticing the arrows and directions, but some will be waylaid from time to time. Your help is of great benefit, but even if it were not accepted, they will awaken and be drawn over and over again to the same truth, much as you have been. There is indeed a Big Daddy in the sky who suggests and leads, but never forces. So rest content and be sure that all is taken care of.

Joyce: So I'd be looking at contentment. Would that include all that would make me happy or would it be boring? Sorry to suggest such a thing, but actually, that's what I am thinking.

Peaceful One: So, is the definition of contentment for you the real question? Thus we come to the true topic of today: Expectations. With what do we all expect to come and go? Today it might be just to rest and recover our strength and resurrect the will to go on. Tomorrow it might be the opposite, perhaps how to get active and enjoy the outdoors and play through the night with new ideas and communications from loved ones on the Internet. So which is right? Should one be given the choice on the wrong day, the level of contentment would be disastrous.

Joyce: OK, I get your point. You are saying that it changes from day to day and probably from moment to moment. So an expectation for contentment must have something to do with filling needs.

Peaceful One: Now we're talking. First, the needs of a person must be discharged in the right order and kind for contentment to proceed. With that in place, we'd like to discharge another duty. How come you don't come to us in the first place so that the fulfillment of needs follow one after the other just as the air you breathe comes ready for the using?

Joyce: I don't get it. You mean that I can ask for my needs to be fulfilled as soon as they arise?

Peaceful One: Or even before.

Joyce: Before? You mean that I'd have food before I was very hungry and rest before I was tired, etc. and never suffer from these needs at all? How can this be possible?

Peaceful One: Now you are questioning the need to be strong of will and to ask beyond the ken of the Conscious Mind to know anything either good or bad. Therefore, we must remind you of yet another thing or two about that mind. Should a mind wish to be at one with another mind, then the first of the minds to be happily fulfilled feeds the lesser and so forth. Therefore, there is great wisdom in finding the greatest sources of contentment that you can and let them lead you in their ways, for they are the greatest and finest. You will receive all that they have, just for the asking. Actually it is more like hanging around and letting contentment into your heart because it feels so good to be there with the Great Sources. So join the party. Let's hear what they have to say.

Joyce: Whom would we listen to who are so content?

Peaceful One: Why Jesus, of course, and Buddha or the great sages who have ascended or descended. These are indeed the greatest of all formerly earth bound sages who have much to offer. Would you like to give them a listen?

Joyce: Yes, for sure. Let's start with Jesus.

Christ Consciousness: Hello, dear little one. Do come close to me and let me put my hand on your back for I know that you are discontent about the shoulder being bothered by a blade of pain. Having accomplished much more than you bargained for, there is the need for me to be with you and vice versa. Just lay down on the floor or couch and I will lend a hand for the healing for such as is my destiny.

Joyce: OK, that sounds good. I've had this pain in my back for way too long. I first felt it when the second Mean One came along. It felt like a stab in the back and I admit that I recognized it as such. However, I did proceed with the relationship and even though it was hell in many ways, there were many things that were great blessings. So I will lie down and let you heal me.

After a brief rest I felt a deep relaxation and thought about being so strong and protected that no intention of harm could ever reach me. It felt good.

Joyce: OK, so what just happened?

Christ Consciousness: Would that you could see me with your physical eyes. I have among my armored friends those with the wisdom to advise you when and where to go so as to never be where danger lurks. In addition, when it lurks and you can take the time to entangle with it for the sake of learning more of me and my protection or for finding a lost one and giving of my guidance. I offer more than sufficient protection from the Higher Mind reservoir of rich and plentiful things to be given away. Would you like to see some of them that have already been given to you?

Joyce: Yes, of course.

Christ Consciousness: In your last relationship, at first, you seemed so strong in hearing of his desire to approach the Higher Mind and thus it was given to both, but both did not apply with the same intention. One gave from the Source of all good intention and wanted to give it away again and again. The other wanted to appear as important as the great ones he admired and thus assure himself a safe passage through life. Thus one was the receiver of great grace and the other karma. It would seem that the possessor of the right intention has all at their fingertips so to speak, but only for the use of the Highest Good for all, never for self-aggrandizement at the expense of another. Thus the most protective device ever given is the gift of the intention for the Highest Good.

Joyce: Oh, I see. If I had not made such a grand intention, then I would have been subject to karma and things would have been worse, but if I had accepted the lesson and turned toward the right intention then the grace would have been given. He could have done the same at any time, I assume.

Christ Consciousness: Quite so. Now let's assume that you had made the wrong decision and only wanted to use another to fulfill your own fantasies of being married and kindly treated. Would another Great One have been sent along to be familiar to you and to give guidance along the right path when you intended to only use him? Not so. He would have remained behind and waited until all was right and only later attended to this duty.

Joyce: I think I know who you mean. This one was very kind and helpful to me. And I did recognize him as someone I knew. He helped me to remain peaceful and avoid much harm. Are you saying that without the right intention, all such help would have been held in suspension until I chose the right intention?

Christ Consciousness: Yes. So did kindness count? You have always been a kind person thinking that others would treat you the same, but it has not always been so, has it?

Joyce: No, certainly not. Some just take the opportunity to walk all over me and add insult to injury. Why is that?

Christ Consciousness: Why not? You were not defended by the right intention for yourself. If you had said that the kindness was to be directed to both your receiver of choice as well as yourself, then there would have been another outcome.

Joyce: Ouch! That hurts me. I've been duped into thinking that being kind is its own reward. I think I got that from the teaching of the church. Was it wrong or did I just misunderstand it? OK, I got it. I used it as a defense, hoping that I would be loved for that quality, but it was a bigger truth, the only source of true love is the Highest Good, none other.

Christ Consciousness: Depending on the intender and how strong they are in self-love or self-esteem determines the good outcome. If they let one deed of harm pass by without objection, then they submit themselves to that harm and all like it ever after unless they stop to consider that it is not working so well.

Joyce: Hmm, I have to think about this. Are you saying that accepting harm is as bad as intending it?

Christ Consciousness: Yes, for all are equal and none are to be given less than another. For now, let's just say that asking for better for both is the correct response. Now let's return to our list of protections given by the Highest Good, for it is the source of much good, don't you think?

From whence did the attorney come who knew the right approach to take for the proceedings to go peacefully and not cater to the whims of a hurt and angry Conscious Mind on either side? Did he not come to mind one night after his usual business hours were over and even answer the phone without a message machine or secretary?

Joyce: Yes, that impressed me a lot. He seemed to care enough to answer his own phone and gave me an appointment the next day. It felt like help and support. His fees were very reasonable. Later, I thought that he should be more aggressive, but he never forced any issue and they all worked out. He just let things play out and the parties involved eventually came to the fundamental reasonable approach of dividing goods and property based on investment and reasonable shares. I can see now that he had peace in mind, not revenge.

Christ Consciousness: Just so. So attorneys are not at fault nor are judges, secretaries or the law in general. Once there is the intention for the Highest Good, anyone can be good, even the so-called bad ones. Do we perceive that the principle here is the importance of the intention and nothing else applies, dear one?

Joyce: I never saw that before, but I see it now. Thank you for this teaching; it will help so many who feel so helpless and fallible. If they just set the right intention, they will do much good and no harm.

Christ Consciousness: Yes, and no judgment need be given to anyone else. Do you remember that the Peaceful One once told you that the Oracles of Delphi who were famous and richly paid for their readings asked only one question of their clients: "What is your intention in doing this deed?" Many would answer that they were in need of gold or fame or the love of another and thus they were told that the venture was fated for demise regardless of the resources applied. However, if the right intention was given, for example, a parent or loved one who pleads for the health and safety of those that they love or want to help, then all was given as positive and thus it was. The oracles were one hundred percent accurate all of the time and thus it is so for everyone at all times.

Joyce: Interesting. That makes doing a prediction easy, I guess, but what does it mean to me and those that I wish to help?

Christ Consciousness: It means that as long as they wish to be made free and you wish to make them free, that you could read them the phone book and they would be made free. The way or the means is never as important as the intention.

Joyce: Well, then I do so wish and intend that all who interact with these writings be made free from fear even without my reading the phonebook. Well wait; maybe I'd better ask a bit more, what else will they be made free of?

Christ Consciousness: Free of the forced consumption of fearful thinking of all kinds. They will stand tall and free of all belief systems whose basis is fraud and defeat of the other. In addition, they will be made free of all self-judgment and limiting thinking. Not all at once, but in time. For the journey is worth the taking for the joy that it produces.

Joyce: I suppose it does me no good to ask how you are going to do this.

Christ Consciousness: Ask away. There are a million stories and many forms of grief and each is attended to in a specific way that is needed or wanted, but the outcome is the same. Highest Good requested always gives good and never harm.

Joyce: That makes me feel happy. It means that I don't have to launch a crusade, an organization or travel around giving classes unless I want to for fun and enjoyment. It will all work out the same, won't it?

Christ Consciousness: You were told that in the very beginning and it is still true and always will be. My sweetest one, you have been indeed cured of the pain in your back as well as the pain in my heart to see you suffer, so both of us have been graced and for that I thank you. Amen.

Joyce: Thank me? I didn't do anything. You are the all powerful wise one. Only you can do this, not me. I should be thanking you and so I do.

Peaceful One returned: And so it is that one and all are the same. You have participated in the intention for the Highest Good and been in the presence of one of the greatest of the great ones, so how have you been treated? How do you feel just now? Are you now content?

Joyce: Once in a while I take a nap and feel very uplifted, rested, and strong and that is what I feel now. I realize that I don't have a heavy duty to perform, or the responsibility of feeling the pain of others and trying to resolve it. That is all done on the spirit side, with my cooperation to be sure, but I cannot do it alone. I think I need a nap. This is a major change in my thinking and my personality. I hope I don't become unfeeling to people's pain.

Peaceful One: What's unfeeling about not allowing them to abuse you but to wish them the best? The rest is for the spirit realm to advise. Just let them be and trust that the Highest Good be given and none else. For now, have a good rest and we will meet on the other side in a dream or two.

An hour later after a nap.

Joyce: Thanks, that felt good. I'm wondering how it leads to contentment. Would you pull this all together for me?

Peaceful One: Oh, most wonderful one. You have won the battle for sure. For so sure are you that you can, with peaceful determination, request and get what you want that you said: "I'll have the Highest Good for sure, no matter what today."

So let's get to the assumption that none is content until all that is wanted is had. Or worse yet, let's say that what is missing will arrive "no matter how long." Contentment is a way to enjoy the reality of the gift many times over even before it arrives or is needed.

It means that one is not a basket case if one is not yet possessed of all that one desires, but rather that the right of obtaining it is sure and the way is clear of all doubt. For doubt to be made clear, there is the clearing away of much of the concern of the Conscious Mind. And that is what you have been doing. Less and less concern has been disrupting your peace these days.

Now let's see if contentment is complete. If one is content, then the possession of yet one more thing is not the true determiner of the peace of the moment. In short, you do not need just one more potato chip. Rather it is the assumption that the direction is good, the way is peaceful and the outcome sure. From this moment on, let's be assured that all that is to come is similar to all that has come up to this time. More good than bad and less harm than anticipated. And so it is that more is to come less and less slowly and with more ease. For ease has been put into the process and not taken back out by doubt.

Now, let's see if more contentment can be had just by being asleep to the thing that bothers us most. As we sit and listen to the music, there is the theme song of all champions for the Highest Good, Amazing Grace. For thee the path is short and good. For thee the three are one. And the last one standing is the first one removed from the fray and brought home to be loved.

So just go about the needed weeks of work and stand free to be happy and complete, for in completion, there is much to be gained and little to be lost. Being in love with the Highest Good takes all of the pain from the gain and grief from the loss. Who cannot be but proud to be the participant of such a grand plan as those described on these pages. Amen.

Chapter Three: Help of a Higher Kind

Dear Reader, how have we come to be so kind to ourselves as to have relinquished our fears? Do you find that you are increasingly less upset with the things that used to cause you angst? Do you find contentment coming into play once in a while even though nothing in particular has happened to cause it? I have, and I hope that you have as well. But exactly how has this come to be with you and me? Have we become better human beings, thinner, richer or more admirable?

Was it just so simple as to stop judging ourselves, which only condemns us to being mean to our own insides? Did we stop critiquing our every thought, motive and aspiration so as to stop the formation of doubt? Was this the most effective thing of all? It does not seem to be much, so how could it have been such a gift wrapped in plain brown paper?

Do you think that the wise one inside of all of us has been helping us to all manner of gifts? At once loyal and selfless and never at odds even with the most plaintive of questions, this inner Peaceful One is amazing at best and a good friend at least. Would that we be wizards of want and expectations, just as the Peaceful One has been, expertly guiding ourselves through the treacherous rapids of confusing thoughts and feelings. How wise it was of us to decide to listen to this One and to ignore the Fearful One. See where it has gotten us?

I must be a nuisance with all of the questions that I ask, but never have I been rebuffed or neglected, thus I must be encouraged and ask again. I am certain that much of what happens to us is manufactured by Higher Mind at our choice. So let's proceed with no caution, for we must be loved. So with no doubt in our minds, we are about to enter even deeper into this conversation.

+

Joyce: Who and when do we come to be Beings of Grace and find ourselves helpless in physical existence with nowhere to turn to make things right for ourselves?

Peaceful One: One has the right to ask such a question if only it were a question and not a fear. For how could you have come at all if you were not a Being of Grace? And with the coming, how could you not have made the enjoyment of the sun and the moon and stars to be your constant reminder of where you have come and are about to return?

Joyce: Are you saying that we came from other planets and will return?

Peaceful One: Are you not curious as to which of the stars you have made home in the last existence?

Joyce: Surely you jest.

Peaceful One: Not one of you is any less than a star in the sky. And so in ancient Egypt we were all depicted as stars in the sky. And so we jest, but also not. Should you have known just how powerful you are, you could have rearranged the stars to your liking as you once did.

Joyce: Are you talking about me? Are you serious? We moved stars?

Peaceful One: How joyful would it be to say that in being a Being of Light that all light is one and since the stars light our way, that not a one of them can be so distant as to not make their presence known. Yes, Virginia, you are a star, bright in the firmament. You can affect much that is to be in your life just by the inclusion of your family of peace on the other side of the great divide.

Joyce: Now you've lost me for sure. I sort of get the part about Light Beings are all the same and that we can see the light of stars from a great distance. But how does that get us to the last statement that we can work things in our lives? And who is the family of peace on the other side? I assume you mean the Great Oneness.

Peaceful One: Let's assume that there is one who wishes to cure himself of cancer but does not currently have the means to do so, so he asks a great doctor to do it for him. Once he is cured, he thanks the doctor and realizes that if they could do that together, they could do much more. Wouldn't you be amazed to see one of us standing beside your bed one night only to bring you your fondest wish? At your request, we arrive each night with yet another item of request. Wouldn't you say that this was a great friendship?

Joyce: Yes, of course.

Peaceful One: Then let's assume rightly that all things are possible if the right help can be had.

Joyce: I guess so, but why would such help be given?

Peaceful One: Perhaps there is an agreement to do so.

Joyce: You mean Spirit agrees to perform certain things in agreement with my request?

Peaceful One: Certainly.

Joyce: Am I the boss or are they? Is this like prayer?

Peaceful One: Both are boss and yes, this is like prayer.

Joyce: Can they do anything?

Peaceful One: Anything at all.

Joyce: Will they do it for me?

Peaceful One: Yes, if you are one with the right intention. Remember the story of the Delphi oracles.

Joyce: That makes sense. If I have the intention for the Highest Good and want no harm and all good, then they can be in agreement with it because that is how their world works.

Peaceful One: Nicely put.

Joyce: Well, let's begin. How do we do this? I have a lot of things that I'd like to ask for.

Peaceful One: Like what?

Joyce: Like no one would ever have to suffer disease. Would they be in agreement with that?

Peaceful One: Certainly. And yes, you have asked for that before and nearly all of those that you wished to be healed were in fact healed. Were you not pleased that the farrier who came to care for your animals said that he had been declared in remission from a very serious form of cancer after very little treatment?

Joyce: Yes, I am very happy for that. He is a simple man who loves animals and his family and I truly wanted him to live in peace so he could enjoy them.

Peaceful One: How about your brother who was nearly killed in a car accident, but he found one last way to escape and merely drove away in the blinding snow storm. Were you not impressed?

Joyce: Yes and grateful, but I wasn't even aware of it when it happened, so I can't say that I asked for it.

Peaceful One: Did you not ask for his Highest Good?

Joyce: Yes, long ago.

Peaceful One: Well, that one request was fulfilled that night even without your knowledge.

Joyce: Wow! I had no idea.

Peaceful One: Well, we have the idea straight from the Source: "Love my children as I love them." And thus we did.

Joyce: Can I ask for myself?

Peaceful One: Of course not!

Joyce: I know when you say "Of course not," that you mean "Of course" and by adding "not" you are commenting on my doubt. So I will state it firmly. I request that I live a long life without any disease, living in joy and happiness. There, how's that?

Peaceful One: Then it is done. So what's next?

Joyce: That's a pretty big request. You mean that I can ask for more?

Peaceful One: If it is in the Highest Good to grant it, yes.

Joyce: How do I know that a request is in the Highest Good?

Peaceful One: No harm and lots of good. Pretty simple really.

Joyce: What if your idea of good is different than my idea of good?

Peaceful One: Then our idea of good will occur as well as yours unless it would cause some harm.

Joyce: OK, I've tried many times to make this work, but I think that I have too much doubt and maybe my Dear Reader would like me to ask for some help to ask with confidence. What could you give us to make this work for many others?

Peaceful One: One device is one that can be utilized as a practice, much like a musician practices a musical piece and can play it from memory without doubt. We will call it an AGOI, an Agreed Gesture of Intention.

Joyce: Do you mean like waving a magic wand and saying Abracadabra?

Peaceful One: If you must jest, we could arrange that, but we have much better and more believable ones to offer. Let's say that you wanted to improve your health, but don't know all of the many ways to make it happen. You could ask us to suggest an AGOI and we would give you an action to do such as drinking a glass of water. Then we would form an agreement with you that when you drink a glass of water with the intention to improve your health, that we will make all of the changes that are necessary to move your health in a better and better direction. After a few years of doing so, the changes would add up to a much-improved human body.

Joyce: Cool. I like that. How about losing some weight?

Peaceful One: If you would twice a day do the yoga abdominal lift exercise three times in the morning and evening before bed, we would make all of the changes necessary for you to promptly return to your normal weight and much more.

Joyce: Agreed. This is easy and so good to have such powerful and helpful agreements. What if someone wanted an instantaneous healing?

Peaceful One: There are those who are doubt free enough to do so by agreement. Isn't that exactly what John of God says happens when he performs his healing agreements?

Joyce: I saw an interview with him and he said that the entities do the healing; he only intercedes on behalf of the sick and injured. He's done thousands of such healings, some instantaneous and some not. So you are saying that anyone can do this?

Peaceful One: Yes, if your heart is pure of fear, judgment and doubt. And even if you are not, there are many who are doing it for others as a way to free themselves from their own fear and make healers of themselves. There are so many ways to heal if only the Highest Good is applied.

Joyce: Wow, Wow, and Wow. So that's why you have been taking me through all of my fears and talking to me about judgments and expectations. You have been healing me of my doubts, so I can be healed and be a healer of others?

Peaceful One: How sweet it is to be revealed. Yes, I will be your partner for all time. Once we have this agreement made and you purify your heart of enough fear, then you can work miracles of the Highest Good just by asking for our assistance by a AGOI or whatever means works best for you. Now let's take some time to rest, for this has been a test of any mind to accept and there is much more to say and to do.

Joyce: How am I supposed to sleep knowing that this is all possible? My mind is full of thoughts. I must ask that all of my readers be granted the same blessing of being able to work miracles for themselves and all others. But most of all, I thank you for being here with me, for all of us. And I am so glad that I decided to let you into my mind and heart and to abandon the fearful line of thinking. I had no idea that it would be this good. Amazing!

Chapter Four: The Travelers

In this chapter, the next events in the life of the Enlightened One are depicted. As she returned to work, she had a traveling companion named Jim who had learned how to channel his Higher Mind and they spent long hours traveling to and from work, which was four hours away from their homes. During these travels, they talked about their experiences on the path to Enlightenment as well as the needs of their families and friends. Gradually, they developed a question and answer approach to talking to the Great Oneness about many topics. Of the many topics that they discussed, we will limit this dialogue to those of the path to Enlightenment, healing and the making of electrical energy from clean energy sources, which was one of their favorite intentions.

We will begin with the day that they discovered their own intentions to be healers for each other and their families, which led them to the direct contact with the ones known as the Great Doctors Group. We refer to the Great Oneness as plural. From these areas of the Cosmos, there are many who reap the vast rewards of being in service. For the travelers on the road to work are just the same as all who have chosen to travel through the universe and have stopped for a visit on the planet earth. Come along for the ride and be sure to leave your luggage of doubt by the side of the road, for there is no grief or pain or illness that cannot be healed by just such a method or at least that's what they assumed and they did not doubt it.

Early Spring Trip

Jim: What's for dinner do you think?

Joyce: There you go again thinking about dinner. You must be burning a lot of calories thinking of ways to have fun. Do you think that you can wait until we get to our exit or did you bring a snack?

Jim: No, I can wait. I was just kidding you. I just love to have fun.

Joyce: I admire that. Some people don't have much fun while living on the earth plane.

Jim: Even as a kid, I never believed that things were supposed to be doom and gloom. I was raised in a religion and I did what I was told, but I never believed a word of it. It never made sense to me. I got bored at school as well. I used to pull pranks on the teachers at school just to get them to laugh. People are way too serious.

Joyce: I am wondering how you came to be that way.

Jim: Don't ask me. I just came as a package deal. What you see is what you get, so to speak. But, my life changed one night on the way home from a concert when I suddenly started to see the insides of people's bodies glowing in bright colors. I took that as seriously interesting.

Joyce: You mean you could see their internal organs, bones and such?

Jim: Yes, in great detail. Some were healthy and some were diseased. I could see them all.

Joyce: What do you mean by see?

Jim: I saw them in my mind as if I was seeing something with my eyes, but my eyes were closed. I think it was the brain's version of sight, not the eyes.

Joyce: How did you feel about it?

Jim: I wasn't afraid, but I was bewildered as to what it meant and so I did some research on the Internet and found that others had the same ability. I found many who were practicing the art of healing through visualizing the body. I knew at once that I wanted to do that type of healing.

Joyce: Had you had any other experiences like that before?

Jim: Not like that, but when I was a child I saw a cross of light in the sky that no one else saw.

Joyce: You said that you were not afraid. Why not?

Jim: I knew that it would be good; that people could be healed by working with the visions and that would be a good thing. I felt a strong impulse to pursue it. Then I lost my job and I had a lot of time on my hands to think. I decided to take some training and start to do it for myself.

Joyce: So that's how you became a Medical Intuitive?

Jim: Yes. I learned to see the inside of the body and then ask to see where it was diseased. Disease shows up as lighted areas. Then I ask for these areas to be healed and when the lights go out, then I know that it is done. It was amazing, but after the training, I knew that something was missing and that's why I came to your class. What you taught explained how and why it all worked.

Joyce: I remember that class. What was most significant for you?

Jim: You said that the Higher Plane always worked for the good, giving guidance and healing and that all we needed to do was to have the intention for the Highest Good and to be at peace. I am convinced that all of the healings that I have seen were completely gifts of the Higher Plane and that I don't have to worry about doing anything wrong, because only the Highest Good will be done. Anything less would not happen.

Joyce: OK, let's talk about intention. Many people teach that thoughts become things. What is the difference between a thought and an intention? Could you channel this answer?

Jim in Channel: One thought leads to another, but without the heartfelt intention to be about something or another, a thought is just a thought. Let one and all know why a thought is different than an intention for there is much confusion on this matter. For a thought to be active, it must be intended to be active. Thus the Free Will is used for the making of one thing or the other to be activated both upon the Higher Plane and the Physical Plane.

Joyce: Great reading. Thanks. It reminds me of a dialogue that I did with the Peaceful One about Agreed Gestures of Intention. It's like a partnership agreement. When you tell the lights to go out to show that a healing is complete, Spirit does it so you know that the healing is done. Ask me a question and I will channel the answer for you.

Jim: OK, let's inquire more about intention. How is a thought activated if fear is the motive? Is it the same if the intention is for peace?

Joyce in Channel: No fear can be projected into the Higher Plane and be effectively activated. It can only be put into motion in the Conscious Mind; therefore it is very limited and easily overcome by the intention for Highest Good. For example, those who intended to cause war in the middle east have done so only because there was the support of many Conscious Minds who wanted to see some peoples dismissed from the area and the United States humiliated. For some, there was the cause to be in control of world politics by means of limited engagements of terror. The resolve to continue to pursue peace, however, has held firm and none who persist with terror will succeed except on a very small scale. Thus we have a good picture of the need to be peaceful outlasting and countermanding the will for the opposite and so it will always be.

Jim: That's so cool. That means that whenever I hear of fear and harm, I should intend peace and it will be effective if I put it into the Higher Plane as well as in the physical plane. It makes sense that if the universe were created to be good, that it would take a lot of energy to do harm in opposition to the good.

Joyce: Yes, but there is a lot of harm that has come to pass. Let's ask about that. Why is there so much fear and harm if the good is so powerful?

Jim in Channel: Why would we support, help and assist any effort of harm? It is only with the help and support of those who believe in the fears and intend harm or at least accept it as necessary that impel harm into manifestation. Without that support, a harmful intention would be but a blip on the screen of life. If, however, you two and many others would ask for the assistance from Higher Mind to delay all harm and make it null and void, thus it will be so, causing a situation that requires even more support for it to be effective.

The work of the next century is to make enough people aware of the need to intend the Highest Good and nullify harm that it ceases to be manifested at all and thus few believe that it is possible or real and it vanishes into non-existence for lack of interest. In the meantime, all are living lives of peace and prosperity and will be unwilling to tolerate even one moment of sadness, harm or grief to threaten their happiness and security.

Joyce: Wow. I can see that there is a plan or path for this to work and it all depends on our intentions. So do I understand an intention to be a thought that has a direction and motion toward an end?

Jim: Yes, I think they mean that there has to be a choice to make something happen. When it is peaceful enough to be given to the Higher Plane, there is nothing else for a Conscious Mind to do on this plane. Spirit does it all. We just make the intention and cooperate.

Joyce: This has deep roots in my life. Even when I was young, I always wanted to know how people thought and acted. I wrote a paper on motivation in college that inspired me to be a teacher and a counselor. I just wanted to understand people and to help. So now I work with employees in a manufacturing plant. Who would have thought I'd end up doing that?

Jim: Maybe we all come prepared to do the work that we as a soul decided to do before incarnation.

Joyce: That means that we had an intention before we even became human. I always thought that knowing one's pre-birth intention was very important to understanding the events of one's lives. I think that is why we have seemingly bad things happen that work out to the good.

Jim: You mean like my losing my job and then discovering that I could heal through visions?

Joyce: Yes, and my living alone to discover that I was communicating with the vast universe of all souls. Actually, that's funny.

Jim: I agree. Actually, I don't have any fear about my life. I know that all that has happened and will happen will be for good. That includes having supper. Don't expect me to answer any more questions when I'm hungry. Here we are at our exit.

Over dinner they talked about the many questions that they wanted to ask including how Jim's wife came to be his beloved soul mate and how Joyce's work at the client company came to be so successful. They shared the stories of their experiences and those of their families and friends. It seemed like there was a whole group of people at the table that night. But as soon as they got back in the car, the Q & A started again and didn't end for two years.

Joyce: Why did I need to be alone so long after the divorce?

Jim in Channel: Your Higher Mind made it possible for you to be in grace instantly after you left the conflict as you requested to be in peace. Much more is to come that will remind you of the grace that you have been given.

Joyce: Thank you. Your turn.

Jim: Why did I suddenly see into people's bodies?

Joyce in Channel: Your vision is a turn of events, which you planned long ago. You are cooperating with it beautifully. You will be a wonderful Medical Intuitive.

Joyce: When did I open to channel Higher Mind and why?

Jim in Channel: When you shared a secret with us. You said that you were not at all happy and you wanted to be so and to be of service for others. With that statement, your life changed for the better and we began to talk to you in a different way so that you could better understand what we were saying. You liked it and paid closer attention. In time, we got better at conversing. You wanted to be the one who can open others to the wonders of the Higher Mind.

Jim: What is a channel anyway?

Joyce in Channel: We thought that you'd never ask, for you are so inquisitive about how things work. In fact, there is a connection between the minds of all in light bodies. It is like lightening bolts reaching from one to the other. Each can hear and intelligibly converse with all others. It is like an Internet highway with everyone on-line all of the time. Just look us up and give us a call, so to speak.

Joyce: Why is a channel so useful to us, but others are so suspicious?

Jim in Channel: Why does a camel walk sideways when someone shakes a whip at it? When one is afraid, one does not channel. One can only wonder at what one has come to know as gifts that others have, but not oneself.

Jim: So fear and doubt are the only limiters? I thought so. The camels are hilarious, by the way.

Joyce in Channel: No, there are many other limiters to channeling, but these are the most common and easily recognizable. What would you have the others do if not be fearful of what they cannot understand and others have told them is crazy? So why do you two trust it, is the better question.

Jim: I knew from the beginning of my childhood that I could do anything that I wanted and the answers would just drop into my mind. I knew that it would all be for the good. Often I made up things that seemed impossible and still they worked. No one wanted to believe me. In fact, that is the one sad thing in my life, that some still do not believe me.

Joyce: When I was young, I knew that others would be upset if I told them what I knew, so I just kept it all to myself. But I kept it sacred and I always turned to it when I was in need of help. I can remember as a child, covering my head with the covers at night and praying for help, and then just feeling better. It was a knowing. Also I had a dream of traveling through space.

Jim: For me it's also just a knowing. Now I see mental visions that are always right. It gets better and better.

Joyce: What are your visions like?

Jim: They are clear and in color like a video and come suddenly and sometimes have action. They are clearly messages or maybe more like communication of concepts or meanings. . .like someone spoke to me and I understood them, but there was no talking. What do you get?

Joyce: I get sentences in perfect order as if dictated and I understand them no matter how unusual the meaning is.

Jim: My wife gets feelings and then she interprets them, asking for the meaning. Sometimes she gets images and visitations from spirit and visions of other forms of beings.

Joyce: So why are there so many different ways to channel?

Jim in Channel: Each has individual tendencies and purposes that need the support of certain experiences, so each is given specific help as needed. No channel is ever left behind, so to speak.

Joyce: That's funny. So I take it that anyone can do this, but in their own unique way.

Joyce in Channel: We'd like to address this question, as no one has the right to take away from any individual their own unique signature or method of opening to channel. When Joyce opens people to channel, she merely asks that we chose the best experience for each and thus each is successful. Anyone who wants to try to open to their own unique channel will be given the same attention and care.

As we left the car to go into the plant to work for the day, we had much to think about and each was asking questions in their own private conversation with the Great Oneness. Before entering the plant, we blessed it with the intention for the Highest Good. All day, we silently asked questions about what to do at work and received wonderful advice of a very practical nature.

It was a blast to be living this way and so much good came of it. I wondered what it would be like to have a whole group of people doing the same thing. How would they be able to work together? They could work together without conflicts or misunderstandings because all guidance from the Higher Mind would be benign.

On the way back home from work, we talked more.

> *Jim:* That was a good day. What do you think was the good that we did?

> *Joyce in Channel:* The Highest Good done today is the openness of the people to do their work without fear. They are listening intently not so much to your words of advice, but the peacefulness of your intention for them. Also, they like Jim's jokes.

> Joyce: You channel the same question and see what you get.

> *Jim in Channel:* The Highest Good today was to be available at the coffee machine for good conversation and to share a good word with the employee who was in grief over her nephew's suicide. How did she know how to think about such a deed unless you had asked her about her family? Your grace in talking about the reality of a self-selected death helped her to be a leader with

her family and to find a way to forgive. Much good was done and much more to come.

Jim: I sure enjoyed talking to her. I could feel her grief and I could hear her nephew talking to me. He wanted to say that he was not happy with his life and wanted to start over again. I gave the message to her that he did not mean to hurt his family. I think that helped her.

Joyce: What a great moment of healing that was. I know so many people who suffer for years over a death like that. You did a good job.

Jim: Let's ask about healing. That's what I'm most interested in. I've taken the Medical Intuitive training and I see many clients. It is so blissful to be able to do this work.

Joyce: I'd like that topic. I'd like to learn how to do it, too. What would you like to ask?

Jim: What is my role in the process of healing?

Joyce in Channel: Your role is to bless the event with the Highest Good and to look upon yourself and the other as Beloved Ones. This establishes the opening. Then you ask the client what they want to be healed of and then go into meditation in your mental laboratory and ask that the healing be done.

Jim: What are the proper techniques?

Joyce in Channel: There are many, but here is one that will interest you. Let's say that the client you saw the other day who wanted to be free of stomach problems was actually suffering from toxins in the system. When you are in your meditation laboratory, turn on your mental screen and bring up the image of a high cliff over looking the sea. Then place an image of the person with toxins on the cliff and ask him to throw himself symbolically into the clean and blue waters below assuring him that he can fly down, dip into the sea and fly back. Let the sun shine on him and watch him to see that he is completely cleansed, but also filled with fresh sunlight and health.

Jim: OK, I'm going to try it now.

There is a long pause as Jim sat back in the passenger seat, closed his eyes, and mentally performed the scene. When he returned and opened his eyes, he spoke about the experience.

Jim: I saw the man standing on the cliff breathing in the fresh air and looking down at the sea. He hesitated, but I assured him that he could fly, so he took off in flight like Superman and laughed. Then he dove into the sea over and over again until he was clean and came back to the cliff. I could easily see that he felt better and he smiled and said thank you. That was great. I know that he was healed.

Joyce: That was great. Let's ask questions about it.

Jim: How are people healed when I am only visualizing it in my mind?

Joyce in Channel: Since all Beings of Light are connected and in constant communication, they can agree to experience in their bodies what you imagine for them. Thus you asked the client what he wanted to be healed of and he gave his agreement, wanting your help. You did your visualization and he participated, healing himself, and then thanked you for your help. It was done with cooperative intentions.

As to the gift of healing, it was given by the Great Doctor Society in the etheric plane.

Jim: Is that a joke? What society is that?

Joyce in Channel: Within the Great Oneness there are groups of beings that delight in giving particular gifts. We have used the term Great Doctor Society as a humorous way to identify they who wish to work with you and your clients to effect healings. Just ask for them and they will respond to anything that is the Highest Good. They promise that it is no joke.

Jim: It sounds so easy.

Joyce in Channel: No doubt about it.

Joyce: No doubt that is a joke but still reality. Let's ask about doubt, for we all have many of them from time to time. Cayce said that doubt is the greatest of all sins. What is doubt and why does it hinder us?

Jim in Channel: Doubt is the perpetrator of so much grief as to have been called the only sin. For if one has no doubt in one's innate goodness, then one would never murder, rape, steal, lie, cheat, be cruel or even unhappy. Take the school shooters for example. Is it not true that it is the most heinous of crimes? So why would one want to do such a thing except to show all just how much hate one has for oneself?

Should one have no doubt that, despite their worldly circumstances, they would be OK if they only rested in peace, the act would never have occurred. But since it did, perhaps it will raise awareness of the need to attend to the needs of those who doubt themselves.

As far as doing healings and readings, the action of doubt is to shut the door to the outer world of peace and to reside within the lonely inner world of fear.

Jim: No wonder it's only the two of us on these rides. You talk about such evil things as doubting oneself. Actually, I didn't realize how harmful it is.

Joyce: Me either. Let's change the subject.

Jim: Yes, I have a personal question. I have healed myself of my own illnesses, but some symptoms still linger. Why is that?

Joyce in Channel: Some symptoms are still a symptom of doubt that you are totally supported by us and by your family. And so we let the symptoms linger a while longer. Should you ever cease to learn from such experiences, we would not allow them, but you learn and ask for more. Thus the causing of one life to be made whole will yield many more to be so. Rest assured that you are no longer ill and such that have been called symptoms are merely manifestations of a want to know more.

Jim: Thank you. That makes some sense. I want to be the healer who healed himself, but I never thought about my family's faith in me being part of what I want.

Joyce: I remember that you said that some do not believe you. I'm thinking that it would be such a celebration if your entire circle of friends and family participated in your final release of the symptoms. I hope that they will come to that realization soon.

I also have a personal question. I have been living alone for a while and I have made many new friends and have been working, but I would like to have a great relationship this next time. What do you get on that?

Jim in Channel: We get what you get. If you do not raise your expectations, we do not want to experience what you will once again have to deal with. Therefore, we have sent you many small experiences of much better friends and each has taught you some of the wonders of open hearts and minds. Stick with us and wait, My Beloved, for we have great wonders for you to behold.

Joyce: I have a hard time understanding how my expectations are too low, but apparently they are, as the last two relationships were not very kind.

Jim: Maybe you doubt that you deserve a great one.

Joyce: No I don't doubt it. I have good self-esteem. I am a good person.

Jim: Look again and see how you can love yourself better.

Joyce: Well, OK, maybe I can do better. Thanks. You are healing me by challenging me to release all doubts.

I wonder if I am to see it as part of what I'm to look for in a new relationship: the ability to heal each other. Wow. Everything is a teaching even in the intimate details of our lives.

Jim: Well, here's our exit to change cars and head for home. Have a good time this weekend and I'll see you on Monday.

Joyce: See you then. I hope you and your family enjoy your time together.

+

Commentary

So much that spirit does is beyond the comprehension of the Conscious Mind, that no one could do any better than to say that they have an open mind to what Higher Mind has to offer. The understandings that are sent are of progressively higher nature as if leading one from one math class to a more difficult one. One learning strengthens and builds upon the prior one. We can't get to the next one without the prior one and so forth. Therefore, the questions and answers are a good way to keep marching in the right direction with total freedom to ask the question over and over again and still get more understanding each time. These are the great lessons that we learned in the car.

We learned how to reliably access the Great Oneness on a daily conversational basis and to engage in so many questions and answers that the Great Oneness became a close family. We talked a lot about healing, as that was Jim's gift. They gave him dozens of healing techniques, which he eagerly learned and memorized, finding them very effective. We delved deeply into how and why, and learned much about why some people healed instantly and some did not. Jim concluded that if a person had done a good job of self-forgiveness and release of fear, that the healings were far better. Those who held their hearts closed with regrets took much longer and had lesser results. Eventually, we found that fewer techniques were necessary and that the most effective ways were the simplest given with the greatest confidence.

I also learned to heal with thought, but my way was very different. It was based on getting around my doubt and it worked very well. I was touched by how loving it felt to do this for another or for myself. It will be described in the next dialogue.

We also began to realize that the intention for the Highest Good works its miracles in the business world as well as for the spiritual path. In fact it works extremely well. Each visit, we blessed the plant before starting work and asked for guidance on how to open the way for the Highest Good to work. As the weeks and months went by, the whole organization began to feel a new hope and energy which seemed to reach certain levels and then break forth into internal actions that were unknown to us, but created so much good that it was starting to show up on the profit and loss reports.

After a year, the company was sold to a holding firm that wanted to reinvest their money because they saw the good that was emerging. The investments allowed improvements that made even more good possible. The good was not just for the profit. It was good for the customers, the vendors, the managers, the employees and even the community. We were amazed. We could not have predicted exactly how it was coming about, but it had all of the markings of the Highest Good. We were grateful and we were having fun. We were making a good living working only a few days a month, learning the secrets of the universe in the car that we called the rolling university. Moreover, we enjoyed watching a company reverse a poor situation into an excellent one. That's a good return for our investment of asking for the Highest Good everyday.

Once we learned the question and answer technique and settled into the routine, the four way conversations provided a great wealth of information and assurances as well as increasing skills in all areas of our lives. It is possible for anyone who wishes to do this to learn it easily. It would take a lot of forgiveness work in order to stay in peaceful contact, but it would be so worth it. The guidance was so loving, wise and even humorous. The grace of the growing relationship with Spirit filled our hearts with wonder as to the great gift that we were witnessing. That is why we shared it with so many and will continue to do so.

Dialogue, Later in the Spring

Jim: We had such a good weekend. My wife and I went to a spiritual group in Indianapolis that does blessings and they were interested in how I am doing the healings. My wife has been asked to become a trainer of their techniques and to teach others how to do blessings.

Joyce: She is such a blessing herself. I don't know that she has to learn a thing. But I know that she will really enjoy it and the organization will prosper because she will do only the Highest Good. It seems to work in any situation.

Jim: Yes, she has tough situations at her work sometimes and she used to get really upset, but now she gets peaceful and asks for the Highest Good and things work out far more easily. One thing bothers her, though. Her car has been dinged three times in the same place in parking lots in the last two months. What is going on with that? We're getting tired of taking it to the body shop.

Joyce in Channel: She is supposed to get a new car.

Jim: What? We can't afford a new car. I just started back to work. She likes the one she has. She will never consider it.

Joyce: That's what I got from Spirit. I don't know how it will work out, but it sounds like the Highest Good at work.

Jim: I'm open. I've learned not to question, I just let things go the way of the Highest Good and I am always surprised at the results. I'll talk to her about it.

Joyce: I want to talk about an experience that I had when I was trying to heal myself of some skin itching. I couldn't get anything to happen so I got the message to ask the blue lady to do it. I saw a mental image of a wispy figure made of dark blue mist with sparkles in the flowing blue mist. She had no face or voice, but I could hear what she meant to say. She was in a small stone cottage in the woods with windows and doors. So I went to the window and tapped on it and she opened it. I put the skin rash situation into her hand and she closed the window and left me standing outside waiting. She never did come back, but the itching is gone. What do you make of that?

Jim: I think that she is your healing self and needs your Conscious Mind to keep out of it because it doubts too easily. If it works, keep using it.

Joyce: I think I will. I think that she has a sense of humor and is pretty blunt. She seemed to say: Go away and leave me alone. I'll call it my Blue Lady Special.

Jim: That's funny. Remember when we were given the healing method for toxin release? I imagined the client diving into the sea and being cleansed. I've been using the toxin release method for a while and it works very well. I have to smile every time because it feels like being on a vacation at the seaside.

Joyce: How many appointments for healings have you been having these days?

Jim: I'm busy every day that I'm home. I set up hours of business and take appointments by phone and e-mail. I charge a reasonable fee for my time and people tell other people so I get referrals. One thing that I really like is that I set the intention that only people that I can help come to see me. If anyone is so skeptical that I can't help them, I ask spirit to send them to somebody who can help and if somebody wants to embarrass or criticize me, that they be prevented from coming. It works great!

Joyce: I never thought of that. What a good idea! That means that we can ask for good experiences in all aspects of our lives and that people who want to disturb us be prevented. Very good! That sounds like the request that we be happy and nothing else. That always invites the Highest Good in and keeps harm out.

Jim: I'm offering a class to teach the techniques to others and have enough signed up to fill the class. It's making me happy, because I'm earning money and helping others to do so as well. That 's a lot of good. I put the money into a savings account and it's growing pretty fast.

Joyce: Maybe that's how the new car can be brought into possibility.

Jim: Of course! See, it was already at work even before we knew we were going to need the money.

Joyce: "Amazing Grace" is playing in my mind. I was reading a book on Karma and Grace the other day and Spirit was saying that Karma is the process that the Conscious Mind needs to guide it to the Highest Good, but the Higher Mind follows the law of Grace.

Oh, I get it now. When you asked for only people that you could help to come, you asked only for Grace and avoided all of the Karma of doubt. I want it to work for me that way as well, so I will set the intention that only people who want and can be helped by my reading ability to come to me and we can all live in Grace. It surely is a lot easier.

Jim: I'm getting hungry again.

Joyce: I'm not going to bite on that one. By the way, how is your energy level doing? Are your symptoms changing?

Jim: Yes and no. I asked for a way to judge my energy level, so they said to use a pendulum on a scale written on a piece of paper. So I tried it and the pendulum swings to the level that I need for the day and I can adjust to what I need.

Joyce: That sounds like fun. We could use it for all sorts of measurements. It might be like dowsing, I guess. I wonder if it will tell us how many miles until supper.

Jim: Don't need a pendulum to know that. It's exactly 12 miles.

Joyce: Why did I ever doubt that you wouldn't keep track of your next meal?

After work that week, we once again climbed into the car to take our long ride home. The car was a ten-year-old road cruiser that was white in color. I had gotten it from the divorce and fixed it up a bit. It had nearly 200,000 miles on it, but ran pretty well, except for a few annoying problems. The cruise control didn't work and the heater would not work in the winter. We blessed it every time we drove it, but we wondered if we could get some information from spirit to solve those problems. We were getting into a whole new area of inquiry: practical and technical questions.

Joyce: I want to talk about the cruise control and how to get it fixed.

Jim: Oh, that's no problem, years ago I worked for a company that built the assembly line that made the steering column for this type of car. There is a ring under the steering wheel that makes contact for the cruise control and other controls to work. Sometimes it wears out and won't make contact. It can be replaced. I will have to take off the steering wheel and get a part.

Joyce: What a coincidence! I would have never thought that I was traveling with the person who designed the solution to this problem. I'll be happy to pay for the part and your time. The principle of the Highest Good is that all must have good returned when they give good, so we need to thank others who give the Highest Good so that it will all be balanced.

Jim: If they had used better metal, the problem would never have happened, but it happens a lot on this model. I'll order the part and have it fixed in a couple of weeks.

Joyce: This car has helped us both to get good work with low expenses. When I got it in the divorce, I thought that I had been given the worst and oldest car, but it turned out to be the perfect one. It is big and comfortable and gets pretty good mileage and is safe. Best of all, it was paid off a long time ago. Except for maintenance and gas, it's free. Another example of Highest Good at work.

Jim: Now, how about the heating. I've checked everything that I can think of, but I can't find the problem. So let's channel for some help.

Joyce: OK, ask the right question and I will channel it.

Jim: In the winter, the car blows cold air unless we turn the temperature up to 85. Why does it do that?

Joyce in Channel: Why does any car give cold air when cold air is available?

Jim: I don't understand that answer at all.

Joyce: OK, I'll ask a different question. What is the process for repairing the heating problem?

Jim in Channel: When air enters into the air ducts, it needs the command to adjust. Do visualization to the air ducts and follow it to the problems.

Joyce: OK, I will try that. I see the air ducts and they seem dusty, but they are all open and air is passing in and out. I'll ask to be shown the specific passageway that needs looking at. It is in the dash.

Jim: That would be very expensive and time consuming to take the dash off and make a repair. I guess we are stuck on that.

Joyce: I agree that I don't want to put a lot of money into an older car, but let's ask another question. I feel like we're not getting the direct answers that we're used to. What is the real cause of the problem?

Jim in Channel: Too much cold air.

Joyce: That seems like humor. I guess we should stop. It's getting pretty frustrating.

A little while later, Jim's wife called on the cell phone saying that it was raining hard at home and their basement was flooding. We were a long ways away from their home. Jim asked a lot of questions and determined which sump pump was not working. He suggested that she unplug it and plug it in again to see if it would start. It didn't. He thought of how he could get home that night to replace it. We both thought of how spirit could help and asked for their direction.

Joyce: Suddenly, I heard the words. " Tell her to just touch it with her hand." I told Jim what I heard.

Jim on the phone: Honey, just touch it with your hand and see what happens. (Pause) I am amazed! She said that it started running. It will be a mess to clean up, but it will drain the water by morning.

Joyce: Oh my goodness! I cannot believe it. The agreement with Spirit really worked on a sump pump! I am so glad that she is relieved and you don't have to worry and try to get home early tonight. This is so amazing. No one will believe this but us three.

Jim finished his conversation with his wife and they recounted how blessed they were by the gift of the repair. I was thinking of all kinds of questions, but we were all just too tired. We pulled in for a rest and dinner stop. After some food and a rest, Jim always resumes his upbeat approach to everything.

Jim: It suddenly came to me that the problem with the heat in the car is that the air conditioning is always on year-round. It does not go off when you ask for heat, so we have to turn up the heat really high to over come the air conditioning. That makes complete sense. I can look at the repair manual and see what the fix would be.

Joyce: You know, it is interesting how we get quick and easy results with some problems, but others are elusive. Why do you suppose that is? I'll ask a question: Tell us why the elusive directions are given.

Jim in Channel: It is not the answer that is elusive. It is the Conscious Mind assuming that it knows the answer and suggesting what it thinks is or is not the answer. The final information happened when Jim was eating, not thinking about it.

Joyce: Hah! That just goes to show the value of a good meal. As long as there are restaurants at every exit, we are in good shape for sure. I wonder what else we could work on.

Jim: How about free non-polluting power for the earth?

Joyce: Really? That sounds pretty big. Do you think that it is possible?

Jim: Remember that the Conscious Mind will think that it is impossible, but let's listen to what the Higher Mind has to say. Clear away all doubts and expectations and just listen. Here's your question: Describe how free, non-polluting power can be given to everyone on the earth.

Joyce in Channel: No power is available now that cannot be charged a fee to produce and deliver. However, there is a plan in place to figure a way for each home to be producers of one's own power from sunlight and to sell it to others in need. Thus, each household will be able to produce enough power from sunlight to serve them and also sell it to others who are in the dark and vice versa. Those in sun help those in the dark and then it reverses the next day. There is still a need for transmission lines and regulation of electricity.

With that in place, there will later be given a very wise way to be within an environment in which electricity is delivered to the very walls of a home or building and to have it vibrate in accord with the wishes of the Highest Good to form a new and better way for humans to live on the earth.

With this we have the right to say that the technology to produce energy at one's home is just about ready to be given, for there are some like Jim and his fellow intuitive engineers who are asking the right questions with the right intention. The intention is to be of use to the whole community of humans without limitations of fear or greed. Therefore, when the technology is available, it will be given to all in such a simple format that virtually any one can go and find an appropriate rock and wrap a wire around it and form the right intention so that electricity will result. With this being said, there are some who have the right to be wary of such statements and so we will relieve them of the knowing until it has been proven. But much more than this can be achieved and will be, just for the asking for the Highest Good.

The intention for the Highest Good for all is so powerful that it will virtually unlock the vast storehouse of information and technology of Higher Mind that has been locked away by greed and doubt for a very long time. It will include the rights of all humans to be free and happy without the harm of environmental pollution or even that of harmful mental thinking.

In addition, for all to be free, it is necessary that each person set the intention for the Highest Good for themselves and to let their brothers and sisters set their own intentions without coercion. For freedom is not the right to remain at large at one's own devices, rather it is the right and the freedom to be made large of mind and for one's soul to rule their own lives in peace and prosperity without intervention of any kind. Without this intention, nothing good will happen. Therefore, we will continue to use the auspices of this one to teach and to portray the many uses and abuses of the greatest invention that the world has ever had: The Intention for the Highest Good. With that we rest for now.

Jim: Wow, that was a long one. I can see that they were very interested in this question being well stated. It leads to so many questions, but I guess that we need to learn the first step, how and why to keep the intention of the Highest Good at the beginning of all of our activities.

Joyce: I remember when I first heard the words: Highest Good. It was about five years ago when I didn't even realize that I was going to go through a divorce and all of the changes that came with it. Actually it was not the divorce that caused the changes. It was just one of the many changes caused by the desire to be happy which have all turned out to be good.

Jim: Well then, let's start with the meaning of the word "good." Here's my question: What is meant by the term good?

Joyce in Channel: What's good is by definition not bad, so let's look at grief and see what it has to say. For most upon the earth plane, there are many confusing and conflicting desires. One might want a car or a house or a spouse or just a million dollars. Let's say that they all want these things because they are all thought to be good. So if good has no bad mixed in with it in their mind, then it is going to be something that they are entirely open to and will eventually have and more.

However, if one part good is mixed with several parts bad in their mind, then they cannot be fully open to it. For example if they want a beautiful new car, but believe that they cannot afford it and need to spend the money elsewhere, then the car is not part of the good for them. However, if another person thinks that they have the money and that the car is all good, then they simply put the thought in motion and at a point in time, they buy the car of their dreams.

The process of finding good is rather a process of eliminating any bad from the situation. In the first case, the better good to chose would be to have more income and to pay off other needs and also have enough money to have the new car. In fact, that is a much Higher Good because it does good in many more ways.

The created universe is loaded with so much good that there isn't any bad except what one thinks is bad. Such limiting thoughts such as I cannot afford it, or I'm not good enough, or I have too many obligations to have fun, or I'm married so I can't make my needs a priority; these are all thoughts that say that there is not enough good to go around, so I have to accept some bad. Thus bad is created for that person and never ceases until they look at the limiting thought and choose another one.

Jim: That sounds like a good way to explain what many books on manifestation are talking about. I learned a long time ago, even when I was a kid, it was more fun to think that I could do something that everyone thought was impossible. It made me feel good.

Joyce: I have a mouse pad with a quote from Henry Ford. It says: "Whether you think you can or you think you can't, you are right." It's a cute way to express this truth. But I want to ask: How do I know if something is good? Sometimes I think: I want something if it doesn't hurt somebody else or if it doesn't take a resource from another who needs it. What about that?

Jim: I don't need to channel on that one. All of those are limiting thoughts which imply that there is not enough good to go around for you and all others to have good things. Try asking that all of the others get all that they want and you do too.

Joyce: That's so cool! Why didn't I think of that? OK, I know the answer to that. Being raised in a big family after the Great Depression and steeped in religious thinking, there was a general societal belief that there was not enough to go around and that doing without was a desirable and necessary virtue. In fact, before Easter we practiced the art of giving up something just to show that we could do it. Actually, I was pretty good at that, and I must have applied that to other areas of my life, thinking that I could not have good things as a matter of principle. Having good things is not good, so to speak. Wow, that explains a lot!

Jim: I was born later than that, but my father died when I was a child and my mother had a big family. She did her best, but didn't have enough time and attention for all of us. But I delighted in inventing and making anything that I wanted. I probably drove her crazy.

Joyce: Your inventiveness was your way to assert that you could have what you wanted. Very good knowing for a small child.

OK, the reading said that there is only good in the universe. Explain that more.

Jim in Channel: The universe was created from a good source, God, and thus only good could be created and nothing else. That good flows like rivers throughout the planets and stars forever, giving and giving and when one of the life forms created by the good returns the good by receiving it and being joyful and thankful, then, the good is multiplied.

Joyce: So having good and being grateful is even better than just one good? Is it stronger than dirt or bad, so to speak?

Jim: Yes, I can attest to that. Bad is miserable and there is no joy in it no matter how you try to talk yourself into it. Good, on the other hand, makes you feel joyful and gratitude comes easily.

Joyce in Channel: Let us propose that there are two simple things that need to happen for a person to be happy. There has to be an exit of thinking that leads to bad or even limits the good. Also, there has to be an inflow of good and the gratitude for it. From this side of life, we see it as two spirals, one going in and the other out of each person's life, so to speak.

Jim and Joyce in unison: What? Spirals? What does that mean?

Jim: I'll take that one.

Jim in Channel: Energy flows and goes wherever it is needed, much like water flowing. Once one says to oneself that one wants to be happy; the soul pulls the plug on bad and it swirls down the drain, so to speak, and also turns on the faucet of the good. It just happens that this is a spiral universe, so the flows are a turning round and round, one way or the other.

Joyce: OK, I know what they are talking about. When I decided that I had had enough of being treated badly and that I just wanted to be happy, within a few weeks, everything bad started to leave my life. The good didn't come in for quite some time. For a long time, there wasn't much left and that's why I was forced to sit at home in the sunny window and think and listen. That was the start of all of this writing and teaching that I've been doing.

Jim: Guess it was worth the wait. What we see now is indeed a lot of good.

Joyce: Yes, and since it was so long without much of anything, I was really grateful for the least little bit of improvement and still am.

We were almost at our meeting point to change cars and each go a different direction, but we had so much to think about, that the miles clipped by rapidly. For me, I saw just how much care and wisdom had been applied to me and my experiences for all of this to happen. My health, my finances, my friends and family and my outlook on life improved and nothing bad ever happened again unless I limited my thinking. It took a long time, but it was indeed worth it.

As I thought about the spiral universe, I remembered that the DNA is in a twin spiral. Also the galaxies spiral outward and clouds roll upward in spiral and tornadoes spiral down. There was something universal about this spiral idea and I had a hunch that it would be further explained as we learned the basic concepts and applied them. But certainly, I felt the hand of God upon my life and I was part of a vast universe of a single principle of good. My fears about what my future held for me vanished because I felt that I was just a part of a vast eternal flow of good. It was a very peaceful and inspiring insight.

Early Summer Trip

We had been making weekly trips to the plant where we worked and on each trip, we had been asking more and more questions. We noticed that we had gotten much better in all areas of our lives as did our client company. We surmised that the Highest Good was catching. Everyone who held it in their heart influenced others to enjoy the good. I looked up the term Highest Good on the Internet and found that Aristotle defined the Highest Good as something that was so good that everyone without exception would want it and nothing would stop them until they achieved it. No one would ever want to harm it or prevent it.

In addition, spirit told me that the Highest Good is so good that it provides all kinds of good that are necessary for one to be completely satisfied. That means health, fitness, friends, family, self-esteem, a good partner, financial security, good work even down to good food to eat and clean air to breathe. Once set into motion with enough strength of intention, such a great good would not falter or end.

All of this is hard wired into the universe and only required the release of fear and limiting thoughts for it to manifest. When it starts to manifest, it comes in the sequence and timing that is best for the Highest Good to proliferate joyfully. There is never a conflict for there is enough good for all and one does not need to take from another to have some. Neither do we need to give it to others, as it will be supplied just because they exist if they can ask for it without fear. We felt blessed to have this teaching and wanted only to enjoy it and to give it away to anyone who would listen. We even asked for the Highest Good for the whole planet and all beings upon it and were assured that all was in motion for its accomplishment. Each trip was amazing.

Jim: Well, I have some good news this week. You will laugh, but I was looking at cars on the Internet and found one that I really liked for my wife and showed it to her. She said that she didn't want to spend money for a new car and would continue to drive the old one. So guess what, she got another parking lot ding. I laughed and looked again and found one for sale at a good dealership so we went to look at it. I could not believe how they discounted the price. It was so beautiful that we decided to buy it.

Joyce: Do you have a photo of it? Wow, that is a great car. That's more car than you were thinking about isn't it.

Jim: Yes, the price was lower than I thought and the car was better. In fact, the savings account from my healing work was almost enough to pay for it. I'll have it paid off in just a few months. It's like it was a total joy.

Joyce: Guess what was at work?

Jim: Yes, I'm going to make a plaque for the dashboard that says: Gift of the Highest Good. My wife is so pleased and her confidence in the Highest Good is much higher than before.

Joyce: That reminds me of how I found my new red car. I had been dreading the negotiations and I hadn't seen one that I really liked. None were red. So I stopped looking and then one day, I was going by a little dealership and just stopped in. There was the nicest salesman who let me drive a demonstrator and I just loved how it drove, but I hated the color and the options were not right.

I sat down in the office and thought about the Highest Good while he looked at the inventory screen to find a better one. He asked me if it had to be red and I said, yes, red, and nothing else. After all, I could just wait a while longer. Why should I take something that I really didn't like? Then he looked a while longer and found one in another city that was red and had just the right option package. It took a couple of days, but I loved the car and the price was way lower than I thought that it would be. It turns out that it was the last day of the month and he made his sales goal and I got a great car. Sweet!

Jim: So we both got a new car. I wonder what else is coming?

Joyce: Whatever makes us happy, I suppose. It will all be in good order but we will have to give up more limiting thoughts. Oh, darn! But then we only have to look at our cars to see why giving them up is a good idea.

A Reading from The Great Oneness

Topic Reading: Enfoldment 12.14.12
Peace and Light Association
Peaceandlight01@aol.com
PeaceandLight.net   Copyright, 2012

Enfoldment is the process of making sure that all is contained in the Greatest Good, thus there is the planting of one seed that is good and it grows and expands according to its original plan. Enfolding is a concept for which there is no need for speed, but should a seed be put in fertile ground and watered and left to the wind and the sun, it would indeed give forth the fruit for which it was designed.

Thus it has been said that: "By their fruit you shall know them." By this was meant that those, whose seed was planted in the fertile soil of the intention for the Highest Good and watered by the firm commitment to accept no less, shall inherit the earth as their own creation. Not as a painter creates a painting, but enfoldment is like a farmer who creates a harvest, all in firm alignment with the principles of growing and harvesting.

Thus there has been seen a new principle unfolding here as there has not been paid much attention to the need to be farmers of the soil of the soul. For one, there is much need for attention to be paid to the need to be raising children according to the principles of the Highest Good. For another, there is the need to be giving and receiving of love as couples do. For another, there is the artwork depending on the inspiration of the spirit only. For others there is the governance of the societies in peace and in justice as to the protection of the rights of the governed to be allowed to be in peace and to pursue their own path to contentment.

If one sees the seed of self-abuse to be reversible, one finds that the DNA winds one way and then another, but it is still the same seed. For if the fine threads of tissues would be unfolded in the right direction, they would produce perfection; if the other, abuse, but both directions come from the same impulse to produce life seeking its own Source. Thus we find that the multiple topics of health, rejuvenation, reversal souls and the like are linked to this one main conception:

Life itself is a replication process of the highest kind of life.

No more or less is implied when we said that the mind is the builder of the life. For once the life force has been unleashed upon the universe, it never again will return without having enforced itself over and over again by the same design. Once this concept is understood, never again will one wonder why a rose unfolds like it does or a spiral shaped microorganism swims the way it does. Never is there grief over the process of digestion for it turns like a screw pulling nutrition in from the mouth and rolling it around turning to the right until it exits in feces. Thus there is much to trust about the universe for all is right and none is wrong unless it is in the leaving process for recycling outward, remaking and returning back in its original form as perfection.

When one first begins their path to enlightenment, they begin to understand this concept and they can begin to open up their minds to receive good. In ancient times, this opening was depicted as open arms on either side of a circle. When this opening to good is found and exploited universally, the earth will be found to be a safe and productive place to be as it is accepted and seen as a blessing.

Once that has been accomplished, then the tight constriction of the fearful mind must be viewed and allowed to fill the space that it actually has, a very small one indeed. For in reality, a fear is only placed in the mind of one willing to be fearful. And as the enlightenment process proceeds, there are fewer and fewer of these available and thus fear is eradicated. This view of one's own mind being in fear is represented in Egyptian art by a circle with a very small dot inside but it can also be seen faintly on one's visual field.

The third and final step is to reverse the turning inward on oneself and to will that grace unfold outward in a right hand turning method according to its original design, which is good, not bad. This is often depicted as the leveling action of a hoe used by a gardener to straighten out the rows of plants or a hook used by a shepherd to keep his sheep on the right path, followed by the luscious use of a stick with several offshoots looking like a flail but which depicts constantly expanding good. When these were placed within the framework of a lesson, they would show the completion of a long life's path or journey in the underworld of earth life under the stars, and the successful access through the mental barrier into the outer world of peace and happiness. And so the Egyptian mummy masks depicted the crook and the flail as the ideal end of a long life resulting in the enlightenment of a mind dedicated to peace.

Enfoldment is also a process for the use of a light beam to encircle an object and to bounce off of all sides so as to make it visible. Even a shard of glass can go beyond that function and break the beams into rainbow colors sectioned in a certain order. The glass bends the light in the right direction thus giving many more gifts of colors to be used. The bending of light is also a symbol of what happens when one asks to be happy. It is an example of what the flail expressed.

With this in order, there is no other than a great mind to align a few things in the right turning order to form the basis of electricity to flow from the right side of an energized crystal enlightened by the sunning of it in vast quantities of sunshine especially on a cool day. Such was the way that the universe was founded for it was said: "Go forth to the right and multiply what good I have given you. And if you wind down to the left in receiving, then I have sent you my Son to show you the right way to go outward in giving." Thus there is both the giving and receiving of good.

For peace and enlightenment is vastly misunderstood unless one needs to be seen as a giver of good and not of bad, for this is the right way. For bad to succeed, it must wind down to almost disappear before it sees the need to unwind in the right direction once again. These are the great reversal events of one's life and once one decides for the good or to be happy, then there is nowhere else to go but to the right turning.

Electricity is also explained as the need for a flow of energy to be directed to the right by a wire wrapped around a core of metal so as to get it going in the right or giving direction. Once this is done, there is much more that can be done, for it forms a magnetic field of attraction and repulsion which educates the particles around it as to where it intends to go and if a line is attached from one end to the other, then the line itself aligns with the intention of the magnetic field and more flow than is imagined is given. Thus the decision to form an alternative current is one in the receiving direction followed by the giving direction and vice versa. One direction follows the other forming a larger and longer field that lasts much longer and goes farther with less energy loss.

Thus it is with life and creation. Once the original intention was set into motion to the right, then a field of attraction was formed called peace. That field has an attraction and repelling nature so that those wishing the good are attracted and those seeking the bad are repelled. To close the door on a bad influence is to say: "I just want to rest in peace." All else that follows must follow the laws of the original intention. To learn that all is in peace unless one chooses to take the recycling path is correct. And, in being correct, there is the need to be much closer to the sunny window idea.

If one rests in peace and enjoys the sun emanating its life force and accepting and receiving it with equanimity, then the meaning of the sunny window is complete. For if one merely rests in peace, then the unwinding of all events in the right direction begins in earnest unless one reverses the process themselves by wishing evil or harm to themselves or others. Should one take the alternating current suggestion, then there is the long line of alternating experiences, which make up what is known on earth as the Karmic Path. Once one is apprised of this concept and it is fully explained and understood, one would never think of alternating, but only go directly to the Source and adopt its intention as one's own and never again have any worry or even threat of worry. For good begets good. And bad only goes for a while until it reverses and becomes good no matter how long lasting it is.

Thus those who have set this long line of experiences into motion have asked that they be set upon the right path and thus it is. With the earth dedicated to the Highest Good, we have a new concept to consider. How indeed did evil enter into the scene? For one to understand that, one has to stand again in the corner of self-concept and perceive that there are two ways to go and only two and one must choose from the two to go in just one direction. Once perceived, there is no end to the choosing, for if one chooses the good, then the attractive forces are so good as to propel you forward and there is no return desired. If one chooses the bad, then there is the reversing back and forth until total confusion and disgust ends the effort and another direction is sought. For one cannot live without good. Only good has life energy. Only good exists. Good tolerates bad only for a temporary solution to the problem of learning to will the good more firmly. Once all on earth are willing to be in the right direction, there is no more use for bad and thus it ceases to exist.

Once one makes this original intention to have nothing but happiness, then many things start to happen. At once, that which was thought to be good, but was really bad, leaves in a hurry and those things that are truly good slowly start to appear. This results in a do nothing period in which rest is most advisable. There is nothing to be had but the good and nothing to lose but the bad and nothing needs to be done because the power of the universe starts to take over. Later, once the firm intention for good has been in place long enough, it takes the form of a magnetic type field in the human aura, which carries one forthwith into a peaceful, healthful and happy lifetime.

Without much effort, there are those whose minds are made up and never turn back, but yet for some, the process can be a long one with frequent stops for yet another grief release. Once one has reached a certain point, the gift of the Golden Thought is given in which one must assert that all of one's thoughts since the beginning of its existence have been turning to the good or the gold and thus there is no resistance even to a bad thought, for it eventually starts and ends in good.

Let's return for a moment to the thought pattern of one who has just begun to choose their Highest Good. Their thoughts enter from the top of their head through the Crown Chakra, which spins, as it ought, in the right direction of peace. However brief it might be, it has set a new direction to the magnetic field that is their aura. Once enough of this thought setting has taken place, which by the way usually happens completely on faith as the events of their lives are still manifesting the bad, then the reversing tendency comes to a stop and all at once there is the thought of the Golden Bough.

This Golden Bough story has as much to do with the setting of the intention of strength as it does the nature of the intention. For from whence does the desire to be whole come, but from the original design of the universe replicated in each and every heart and soul? Thus it is engineered into the mainframe or hard drive of every nerve, bone and muscle of the human body. Thus it has a much stronger response to the good than the reverse has to the bad, which takes much longer to manifest. Thus with just one burst of: " I told you so, this place is just as good as any other," the heart, mind and body start to resonate to the tune of "Happy Days are Here Again" and thus the body heals and rejuvenates itself.

With that being said, there are a few things that can be done to facilitate it moving in the right direction and to keep it there long enough for the forward motion to become a pulling rather than a pushing with effort. First the heart must hear the beat of the different drummer to be benign and kind without any harm. Thus the heart opens. Secondly, the help must be different than that first conceived by the Conscious Mind for it to be believed that the Conscious Mind cannot create the better result. Thus the mind opens. Finally, the hand on the till must be better than the one that the Conscious Mind has had. Thus the impulse to act hastily stops.

Once all of this has had time to play out, there is yet another matter of the release of toxins within the body to address. For one who has had toxic thoughts must have toxic blood. For these to be released, there is the need to allow the releases to occur without concern. It can be anything from lots of sneezing, itching, coughing, stomach cramps, temporary mild diarrhea or even hair loss. Even lesions on the skin can come from this source and any doctor aware of this process can help with the mild cures such as Cayce recommended and assurances that this too shall pass followed by counseling as to the good that is ahead.

Then there are energy passages that need to be made open such as the heart valves, the alimentary canal, the breathing channels, the skin, the cheeks, the mouth, ears and all organs of expression. If any of these seem to be in undue distress, seeking of help is appropriate as long as it is not to address the problem with the addition of even more toxins of thought or substances. As these passages start to stabilize in their ingoing and outgoing processes, there is much to be gained in the stability of joy, for the person no longer feels so tired and depressed or sick.

As this proceeds for a long time, there is the passage of the event of High Consciousness to have made its advance in the form of a splash of raw energy to the field of vision. For many see spots that are of colored light that are very bright, or wide streaks which run across their field of vision. These are indeed the infusions of grief relief followed by the giving of much grace from the human aura. As far as we can see, there is no retreat from this point, for these tubules of light in the aura are indeed indicators of the need to be pointed in the right direction upon the etheric plane. Those in the Etheric Plane have been sending special healing treatments of the highest and most unique kind for each mind, heart and body which are as special as one's own dreams. For all of this to happen in such a sequence and such rich rewards to be had, there must be a plan for the keeping of all things to be whole and safe in the protective care of the Highest Good. And thus it is.

With the rights of being included within the Great Quietude of the Oneness, one might even be said to be included within the womb of the great Queen Nut, depicted on Egyptian walls as a long slim woman who hovers over the earth dispensing the goods from the great storeroom of grace, so to speak. She is the translator of many requests and the bender of light so to speak, to offer the blessing of the rainbow of gifts. For it was she who cooperated with Bet to form the most high ones' entrance into the great unknown shown as a doorway to the stars.

With this we are ending this treatise, for this one is excited with the news of such a simple, but powerful way for her to be made whole as well as to help all others to do the same. And so we will be made replete with the news that the birds are singing and the sun is shining and the tasks need doing, all with the light and joyous heart of one made whole, or at least made known that she was whole in the first place, the middle place and the ending place. Thus all three of her questions have been answered for she is a Beloved One come from the Source of all Love, living within the constraints of time and space but for a time, totally in love with herself and her true nature and she returns whenever she wishes to. Amen.

+

Joyce: I am sitting once again in my sunny window after a long week of work, relaxing and feeling tired but happy. I am reminded of how my life has slowly grown more secure, peaceful and productive. There is an ease and contentment now. Not contentment with things as they are, but content that all that unfolds is much the same as before only better. Now that I think of it, I'd be better to call it trust.

What it is that I am trusting is not the cause or the effect of something added to my life, but rather the uncovering of something that was always there, just hidden from my view. It was hidden by frightening thoughts and actions, which took my attention away from the moments of enchantment that I am enjoying now. How close it all was to me all of the time is the teaser. How little it was hidden is now ridiculously obvious, like a pink Easter egg lying in the green grass. Dear Reader, it is with such joy that I welcome you back and invite you to partake of a few more lines of dialogue to discover for yourself where it all lays in your life. So let's begin again and go line-by-line and I will tell of the wonders that I found doing nothing while sitting in a sunny window. And I have to begin with right now, for it is so beautiful and full of wonderful peace. I want you to experience it with me, to be sure. So let's start.

Joyce: Peaceful One, I am here with you and you with me. I sense your presence. My body feels soft and gentle, with many feelings of bliss rippling over my skin. I feel the softness of your breath and the gentleness of your heart. I know that it is you, or rather we.

Peaceful One: How soon we became one is entirely dependent upon the opening that you give me to enter into the room of your soul's intention to be of service and to give you the gifts of a wholesome life, a secure future and moment after moment of peaceful bliss. It was not I; it was you that brought you this moment. Or should I say we?

Joyce: I can hardly believe that what you say is true, but it must be. Explain to me again, how I came to be so blissful.

Peaceful One: Do you remember how often we sat together and dialogued about the nature of your relationships and the events of your life, both the good and the bad? In all cases, there was no care too great or sorrow too deep to be discussed. How honest we were with each other. Indeed, the most viable part of our relationship has always been the communication. It is only recently that you have noticed the feelings of my presence in your body.

Joyce: It is the relationship that I've always wanted to have.

Peaceful One: What relationship could you effectively have that wasn't safe, gentle, loving and helpful?

Joyce: I never hoped that, in any lifetime, I could expect to have relationships that good. I guess I thought that any relationship had pain and difficulty. Isn't that right?

Peaceful One: One that we initiate is never sad, hurtful, painful or difficult. It is only soft, tender, healthful and fun, so which one would you like to be in relationship with is the real question.

Joyce: Do you mean that everyone has a Peaceful One and a Fearful One and being in relationship with their Peaceful One would be a blessing and the other a painful one?

Peaceful One: I couldn't have said it better myself. Maybe I did. So from which mind are you speaking now?

Joyce: Well, I guess the peaceful Higher Mind. Oh, I get it. When I am in that mind, I can hear you and all of the others and am in peace, so I would always say what you would say and give myself an experience of a relationship that is peaceful. Interesting.

Peaceful One: Let's say for example that one who has had a road trip of Conscious Mind fate has entertained much grief and wishes to come into relationship with you. Which of their two minds would you rather have?

Joyce: OK, I get your point. A grief filled Conscious Mind would be very dangerous to be in relationship with. It might start out looking good, but as soon as a fear is triggered, then the fears come rushing in with the intention to punish, protect, blame, destroy, lie and all the rest. Sounds like some that I've had.

Peaceful One: So many are like this that no one in their right mind would want one without some assistance from the other mind. Therefore, there are many family arrangements that foster only the Higher Mind and discourage the Conscious Mind. These might be like taking care to bring roses on Valentine's Day, observing birthdays with joy and making a vacation to be a relaxation of the stress of both minds at work to make a life. The best that can be had is that as one advances in wisdom, one learns to forgive and forget much that is said which is sad and hateful and focus on the good and beautiful. With much stress and effort, many couples come to an understanding of how the Highest Good operates: no harm and much good.

Joyce: I don't know why or how it has come to pass for me that I cannot find another who would like to invest in such an effort in honest dedication, but that has been my life path. Would you guide me on this matter and teach me how to have a relationship without pain or suffering and giving great good?

Peaceful One: Of course, you would have to sit for many a day in that sunny window and release much of the fear that has plagued you most of your life. Would you be willing to do that?

Joyce: Of course, I already have. It makes me happy to live without fear. I feel free to be happy for the first time in my life. Why wouldn't I want that?

Peaceful One: OK, then, would you be willing to always be in your Higher Mind and to have nothing touch you that was sad or harmful for the rest of your life?

Joyce: Yes, of course. Wouldn't anyone if they only knew how?

Peaceful One: Then we have a course begun and completed in one sentence. If one releases much fear and lives and speaks from their Higher Mind most of the time, then they are highly qualified to be relationship masters, for we guide their discussions and soften and bring joy to their feelings.

Joyce: You mean to say that being in a relationship with such a one would be to hear the Higher Mind speak and respond most of the time?

Peaceful One: Yes, of course. Just as you are doing now. How beautiful it is to just be joyfully occupied in being in

Higher Mind with each other while all else comes beyond expectations to be beautiful and good!

Joyce: You mean that I don't need to do anything else? Just do what I'm doing and all will come in happiness and bliss?

Peaceful One: Yes.

Joyce: That sounds like doing nothing and getting everything, just like after the divorce. Will it always be like that?

Peaceful One: Oh well, if you want it to be hard just give us a call when you return to your Higher Mind.

Joyce: Of course not!

Peaceful One: Well then, let's get on with the next step of this discussion since we are already begun and done in the same breath, so to speak. In what part of our discussion did you not learn of health, good will to all beings and the grace of acceptance of yourself? Let's see if I can ask and answer the question as if we were one. You would say, "In all cases, of course, and I am the better for it." Am I right?

Joyce: Yes, you are right. That is what I would say. Why are you answering for me?

Peaceful One: For once in agreement about the Highest Good, there is at once no conversation at all, for we are one and constantly expanding through good following good. How's that for worrying that a good intention can be given and not received in return?

Joyce: Oh, I get it. Once two people are both in their Higher Minds, they are one in thought and don't even have to discuss much. They'd be in peace. But what happens when one leaves the Higher Mind and speaks from the Conscious Mind?

Peaceful One: If that would happen, then once or twice a day, one would ask for relief from all harm and request only good. For as much as one intends to be in Higher Mind, the Conscious Mind still needs attention to heal. Thus we have the convenient option to remind each other. That literally means to re-mind, or request that they change from their lower mind to the higher. Barring a capable response, there is always some form of time-out.

Joyce: I think that I like this. You mean that if my partner in any relationship said something mean, that I would remind him or her to reconnect to Higher Mind or to take a time-out until they can. So I wouldn't have to take mean behavior and endure it. I'd only have to recognize it for what it was. Cool, I like that. But wait, that would imply that both clearly understood what Higher Mind was and how to get there and stay there and agree to the terms of the relationship from the beginning. Right?

Peaceful One: Right you are.

Joyce: So not just anyone could apply. Only one who has taken the time to shed some of their fear and to learn how to stay in Higher Mind?

Peaceful One: Or one who would wish to do so by being in relationship with such a one.

Joyce: You lost me there. Wouldn't one in Conscious Mind spoil all of the peace?

Peaceful One: What is peace if not productive of more peace? Should one of Conscious Mind come in contact with one of Higher Mind, the higher of the two would influence the lower and glad to say, that's how the cookie of fear crumbles. As soon as there are a few who prefer a state of Higher Mind, then there are a few more and so forth. Did I not say that where one or two of you were gathered, that there indeed am I?

Joyce: Oh, you must be speaking as the Christ Consciousness.

Peaceful One: Not exactly, but if I am of the same mind as that Great One, then I speak with that mind and we are one and the same as of one mind, so to speak. Thus as the Father says, and I say the same thing, then I and the Father are one, to quote another fine speech.

Joyce: So are you implying that the Christ Consciousness would reside in every relationship that is dedicated to being in Higher Mind? Wow, that is a wonderful thought!

Peaceful One: Why stop there? Is there not a holy one or great one in each person's spiritual family tree to quote or to use as a guide? How wide is the word Vast Oneness?

Joyce: Pretty big. So where do I fit into this?

Peaceful One: Are you not I and me and thee and thou? Yes, you say. Then why not just be peacefully blissful while I fill up a cup of water and let you think about that.

Joyce: Oooh kaaay? I'm losing one of my two minds, I think.

Peaceful One: There you go taking my thoughts and saying them aloud. How can we have a discussion if you are always jumping ahead to the end? (in humor) Yes, one does sense a loss of identity as the Conscious Mind defines it, but it is a good thing. Soon a new identity forms as one mind grows into being at one with the other. It is like a high school graduate who has to change his or her identity from being a high school student to being an independent adult. Edgar Cayce once said: "We don't go to God, we grow to God."

Joyce: I want to go back to something you said earlier. If one party to a relationship is in Higher Mind and the other Conscious Mind, how does the Higher Minded one stay there and not be drawn into fear by being treated meanly?

Peaceful One: How would one do that if they had no fear to influence them? For fear from another is not the same as fear from within. That which is given or suggested from another can be resisted by merely looking at it and discarding the false suggestion. That which is within is a horse of another color.

Joyce: So that's why we should take much time to shed our fears before entering into any relationship, right?

Peaceful One: Anytime there is need to be in greed for speed, there is the opportunity to save one's grief just in case one might need it for yet another trip through disaster. Why do you think that you have been here so long without any company? Do you think that we have been depriving you of needed support or punishing you for being bad? For shame, we would never do that. It was only for the purpose to cleanse away enough grief so that you will never need to fear any relationship for any reason.

Joyce: You are teasing me, but it is the truth. Yes, I felt all of those negative feelings about being alone, but I see now that the purpose was an excellent one. Actually I often thought that I was alone because I was at fault and had not done things right or maybe didn't deserve better.

Peaceful One: Why would you think that about yourself?

Joyce: Well, I guess I was afraid.

Peaceful One: Of what?

Joyce: Oh, this is hard. I think I was afraid of someone else coming along and saying: "See I told you so" or worst yet "What makes you think that you deserve this?" It is just too heartbreaking a moment, so I just accepted that I was not going to get what I needed and should be humble like the others, so I wouldn't have to experience that painful moment.

Peaceful One: Who told you that?

Joyce: My father at a birthday when I was a small child, but he said it jokingly and I know that he loved me so. I was a little girl and very sensitive. Actually he probably wanted me to be strong and answer back: "Because you love me and give me beautiful presents."

Peaceful One: How right you are. Your small child mind did not hear the rest of his intent. For he did in fact give you a birthday gift, didn't he?

Joyce: Yes and with a big smile on his face. For he and I really loved each other.

Peaceful One: Well, then admit nothing but that. He loved you for he was in his Higher Mind when he was around you. His life was a hard one of responsibility with a big family and an important job. But when he came home and listened to his beautiful children, especially you, he was happy and very proud. So now listen to your name for yourself. What do you hear now?

Joyce: I am a good one in a good family and well loved just as it should be.

Peaceful One: OK, then what happened next that convinced you that you could not be found among the best?

Joyce: When I was a teenager and young adult, I could not find a young man who really liked me that I also liked and admired. I remember thinking that I would never find one that perfect, so I'd better take what came along.

Peaceful One: So what is admired all about?

Joyce: Well, admired means that I find someone my equal or better and I can be proud to be with him. He would have a strong character, be a productive member of society and a good, loving man who can be trusted.

Peaceful One: Then you did in fact think that you were special and that it would be hard to find another of your equal? How much does that say about your basic self-esteem?

Joyce: You're right. I knew that I was special, but I had no confidence that others would recognize it. I tried, but I didn't find such a one. Why?

Peaceful One: Because right and wrong came in between the two of you. Your Conscious Mind distorted the intention to be whole once again. If you had stood firm in the desire to find one so intentioned, he would have come along in time. It was only the fear that it wouldn't happen that lead you to an unwise choice. Do you see how fears are not reality, only a produced negative expectation that can distort your true being and derail your happiness? You have the choice to accept it or not. It is within you. It's not real until you make it real.

Joyce: OH! You mean to say that all of this time and trouble are due to a wispy thought of disaster that became true because I didn't resist it. Wow! Now I do feel like a fool.

Peaceful One: No fool like a fool who finds the truth. Yes, each fear is a decision point pointing in the wrong direction while the little white rabbit is showing up all of the time leading Alice into the garden of truth. She almost missed it because she had a lot of pressure to accept the fear as truth, but in the end she left the scene that was being portrayed to her as real and entered Wonderland. The same is true of Dorothy who didn't want to face life as an orphan, so she dreamed of another place called OZ where she found her courage to be part of a new family. Both were great journeys of literature as well as truth.

So, as we have this new book called **Walk to Freedom**, let us both make a pact. Do not let any fear destroy what you know to be true. You have a right to be happy and no guilt, sorrow or blame can overpower that. Go right ahead and be happy in every circumstance because in all of them, I am there with you and can make everything that you need come to be available even before you ask for it. That goes for all of those readers that you love as well.

Joyce: Really?

+

Dear Reader, I am so glad that you are reading this with me for I am having such a different experience in this book than the first. How am I going to understand all of this without you? Are you asking the same questions that I am? Even though you have learned to avoid doubts, do you sense the edge of your normal thinking looming ahead like the roadrunner screeching to a halt at the edge of a cliff? Do you think about jumping off that thought cliff and learning to happily fly away; then coming to your senses and thinking: "Don't be absurd, there's nothing there to support me." "Who could it be that could support me both on solid ground as well as in thin air? "

And so we sit in the light of a sunny window and wonder about our lives, you and I. Could hope be a fool's way to describe what we always were already? Really? Could it be us, ourselves, our Peaceful One, a part of ourselves, who would support us anywhere we wish to happily go? Was it just our fears that convinced us that we had no power to do so?

OK, I hear your Fearful One saying: "Stop that, or I will put this book down and never again pick it up. Then where will you be without me? At least I will be safe, I don't know about you. You are headed somewhere I don't wish to visit."

But really now, just how well has it been working out for us to stand in the shadows? Do the shadows comfort us? Amaze us? Entertain us? Heal us? Prosper our efforts in all ways? Do they tell us the truth and seem like home to us, or are they just apparently safer than the alternative?

Are you with me now as we move on? After all, you can say, its just words on a page, not real life. Come walk with me and we will find our way together. It's got to be better than living in the shadows of fear.

Chapter Five: The Runaways

As soon as I sat down today to start a new chapter, I got a phone call from my neighbor who told me that my two mules had escaped the pasture fence and were running down the road. This almost never happens, but today it did. I bundled up in warm clothes and got my halters and lead lines from the barn, running down the road. My neighbor had found them together grazing on forbidden land, but at least they were standing still. We tried to approach them but they took off running again, this time toward the barn. But first they took to the road and had cars stopped both directions to avoid them. I was walking up behind them way too far behind to do much good.

A woman and her daughter stopped and got out of their SUV and tried to approach them. The mules shied away, but by this time I was catching up from the opposite direction and we had them between us. They kindly gave up and let us catch them. While we put halters on them and hugged them in relief for their safety, I thanked my neighbor and the strangers on the road. It turns out that the daughter had taken some 4H programs and knew a little about handling animals. They were happy to help. People in the country are so good and helpful to each other. I was so grateful to them for their help.

I led the mules back to the barn and found that the fencing had fallen down in the mud, so I tied them inside the barn and locked all of the doors. They could not be allowed outside until the fence was repaired. I gave them fresh hay and water and petted them, offering some carrots. Next I called for my farmer who sharecrops my hay. I pay him to help me with my farm work. He was not home, but I am sure that he will call me as soon as he can.

All is quiet for now and I'm sure that it will work out just fine. I rest and think about the experience. If it had happened several years ago, I would have panicked and doubted that I could have handled it myself. I would have imagined two carcasses dead on the road. But this time, I was sure that it would be fine and resisted all fears. In fact, so much perfect help showed up that the escape was all short lived and it was even enjoyable to experience so much help and support. It makes me wonder just how far I have come.

Joyce: So what did you think about the Great Escape, dear Peaceful One?

Peaceful One: It's not what I thought or you thought, but what you didn't think. You did not give into the fear, so you kept your Higher Mind on the job so to speak and all worked very well. All except the two dear ones in the barn. They would like to come out in the sunshine once again.

Joyce: I'll bet they would! Sorry, we have to wait for some more support before we can do that. Until that fence is repaired, they are in lock down. Actually, the amount of support is the most amazing part of this experience. You say that the Higher Mind was the on the job. So what did the Higher Mind do?

Peaceful One: Your Higher Mind was in love with the idea of a safe and prompt return to the safety of the farm, so all others who saw the incident were as well. Even the graceful dear ones. Once thought to be less than cooperative, mules are actually very intelligent and loving animals, as you have found.

Joyce: Yes, they are my best friends most days. That's why I keep them. I feel peaceful around them. Oh, I get it. They are in Higher Mind as well.

Peaceful One: Of course. Do you think that the Father would make any creature to be mean and to live in pain and misery? All of God's creatures, both great and small, are Beings of Light and are to be treated so by anyone who has any access to their Higher Mind.

Joyce: I'll vote for that. They have taught me more about unconditional love than many humans. Too bad they don't communicate with words.

Peaceful One: There you go putting limitations on good. It is a foolish attempt to be sure. In fact they do communicate just as I am doing over spirit.net so to speak. You can go to: Animals @spirit.one and ask for them to speak.

Joyce: Really? OK, Itsey, speak to me.

Itsey: What do we want more than anything else? We want to be wanted by you. So do be about your business, but let us bless you with our warmth, contentment and love from time to time. Did we bliss you out this morning or what?

Joyce: Yes, you did. I am so grateful that you let us catch you and bring you home. I promise that I will visit you more often. How's Daisy?

Itsey: She's standing here right beside me and is a bit disconcerted that you did not address her first, for she was here on the farm before me and thus she is to be given respect for that. At least that's what she thinks. I think that I'm much smarter and prettier.

Joyce: You two are sisters for sure, bickering back and forth. Tell her I loved her first and yes, you are the prettier of the two. I promise that I will get the fence fixed and let you out as soon as possible. You two are gifts of grace given to me for comfort and a graceful example of Highest Good.

Peaceful One: See how easy that was? Was Itsey Bit her true name or is it Beloved One living in an animal body?

Joyce: I see what you are saying. Animal souls are just as beloved as any, maybe more because they don't seem to suffer the fears of the Conscious Mind. I often joke that if we humans could love half as well as a dog can, that we'd be Divine. Do animals have Conscious Minds?

Peaceful One: Yes and no. They have an animal mind which is different than humans. They come to this existence to be beings of strength with only one mind of the Higher Mind, but also with a herd, pack or group family mind to associate with the physical plane. With the group animal mind of their species, they live in peace and prosperity and all are happy in their experiences, much like humans of the future will do.

Joyce: Do you mean to say that they are more advanced than we? That is a good laugh on behalf of what society typically thinks.

Peaceful One: Not so much more advanced than humans, but they are excellent as companions on the earth experience journey. You are about to ask about animal cruelty and the eating of animal flesh.

Joyce: Yes I am. I need to know the truth about this.

Peaceful One: Then I shall tell you the truth as I always have. Not one of the acts of cruelty committed against an animal was accepted as such. They all know what type of being they are and none suffered beyond their desire to experience themselves as animals. Most just left for yet another existence long before the cruel end took place. Their bodies might be standing, but their experience had ended.

Those who committed the cruelty were both the perpetrators and the victims for they knew not what they were doing. They were separating themselves from their own Higher Mind and that of a blessed animal come to love them. Their end is cruel indeed.

All other animal behaviors are explained by the need for one to give and receive resources or to procreate, as is their nature. So no use trying to persuade a snake not to bite you when you intrude on its den, or climbing a tree to escape capture from a lion that is hungry for meat, for their specie behavior is explicit.

And in case you are wondering why one decides to be taken for dinner by a predator but not another, let us assure you that it is all worked out in perfect timing. One to be made fat and the other lean is the give and the take of all things. The Native American Indians had it right. Before a hunt, they would ask the spirit of the right deer to come forward and announce itself as the giver of the day and to let them take it for meat. Then they thanked the deer and enjoyed the meal and the life force left behind by one who danced around the fire with them in peace. Now that is not to say that animals raised for slaughter is a good thing, because they lack the freedom to chose to give their gift of life, but remember that those animals have the protection of their Higher Mind to depend on. Hunting is all about the need to experience the gift of life. All in God's way is the rule for all beings.

Joyce: Interesting. I wonder how the animals view us.

Peaceful One: Not a one of them is without peace, so let them be is the usual rule. But a few of them enjoy domestication and thus they become close contributors of food and love such as for work, eggs, fur, feathers and hides. Such is the agreement and it should be kept so for they have left their natural instincts largely to the background and therefore they must be as well kept as possible. Certainly not let to run down the road as this morning demonstrated. Actually, your beautiful mules let themselves out for a short run and had every intention to return, for your farm is a delight to them and you are part of their family.

Commentary

This discussion about animals was such a surprise to me, but I can see how animals are also part of the Great Oneness, incarnating with animal species minds, doing their own thing, so to speak, to be part of a peaceful earth. I think that we should be so grateful for their presence. And apparently, they are here with the agreement that, at times, their bodies will be used as a food source. I thought about the same for plants. They have come to support us, love us, inspire us and in short be companions on the path of experience in the physical realm. It would only be natural that we do the same for them. Yes, it is a true Higher Mind relationship just like the one I was asking about with a partner. Hum!

    I don't see why we shouldn't use our Higher Minds to communicate with them and to ask about their care. It would be interesting to see how that would help those who are in the veterinary health care professions. I would think that each animal could very competently ask for the care that each needs and wants.

    However one feels about eating meat, most animals have short lifetimes and prey on each other, and apparently Highest Good protects them perfectly. Perhaps our role is to be in cooperation with the intention for the Highest Good for all beings on the earth, including animals. I would think that observing them in their natural habitat would be like reading an encyclopedia of how Higher Mind gives and receives life. But most of all, I think that there is much more to discover about animals by listening to them and that those who particularly love them would have a very good time doing so. May we all proceed in peace with all animals.

Chapter Six: The Soul's Progress

Although it was a day much like any other day, there were none to be had that gave me more clarity on why I am here and what I am doing than this day. It is March and the snow is gently falling in big heavy flakes. It made no sense to me as to why I would be here at this time of my life, single and living on a farm, miles from my closest relative or friend, but yet here I am.

Have you, Dear Reader, ever wondered the same thing? What am I doing here or better yet, if you believe in the choice of a lifetime: "What was I thinking?" I wondered about it a bit and then a message came in from the Peaceful One who is now showing up with the answers before I can even ask the question, as any good friend would.

Peaceful One: Would that you have found a question that we could answer with ease. For this simple question of "What was I thinking?" will indeed involve a lot of time to understand. It is by far the most complex issue that any human can attempt to grasp, but it is indeed the most profoundly enriching one to attain.

So let us take you back to when a person is born and give a reading on the matter:

A Reading

Topic Reading: Making Progress on the Spiritual Path May 24, 2012

>Peace and Light Association
>Peaceandlight01@aol.com

    As a soul enters into human form as a baby, it does so in the state of incomprehension as to what kind of a being it is, either from the physical form or the spiritual. It cannot know how to walk or talk, neither does it know that it is a part of God for it cannot conceive of much beyond eating and sleeping. From this point, it then progresses little by little from one state of understanding to another, highly influenced by parents, experiences and the current society. As one begins to understand how walking and talking occur and begins to perform these feats, there is joy and a sense of being a much higher being than was previously thought. As adulthood is approached, there might be others who can outperform them, so a sense of urgency is allowed for the purpose of expanding self. Thus the discovery is made that even in adulthood, there is much to be learned and advancement to be had.

    And yet, there is still an enormous area of exploration that is often left to a few who call themselves psychic adventurers. Should a person decide to explore themselves beyond the visible and concrete realities, there is a universe of great cause to be had. It was in this way that Edgar Cayce was sent to be a pioneer of sorts. He alerted the world that such feats could be done peacefully and easily, even in one's sleep. With that there are many benefits to be gained such as the learning of how the body can be healed, the existence of past lives, the history of the earth and mankind and much more. It is for this one to pick up what he left behind and to explore those high grounds even further. And indeed, we are inviting all others who wish to explore it to follow in these footsteps.

Although much is to be realized, there is also much to learn about gaining access to this high ground and what there is to explore when one gets there. As for the access, there is a portal of fate that can be crossed very easily just by being peaceful and measuring one's fate against the unknown instead of the known. And so for the measuring of one's courage, let's just say that it is easier than falling asleep but much more challenging than staying awake.

And so with the ground being accessed, there are some rules found to be in place. First, there is the name of the Source from which the flow of energy called The River of Life derives its direction and energy, which is God. Then there is a need to be in contact with and in conversation with the Source. In short, there must be a question followed by an answer. If something is offered, it is not known if it is suitable unless the receiver says that it is or asked for it in the first place. And so the beginning of the Long Story states that none but God was present in the first place and in finding this place to be happiness itself, God wanted to find a place to give it. And so souls were created so that they could receive love, be love and be returners of love. For this to happen happily, there must be the happiness potential of doing it all of the time and even in different times and places. Thus there was a need for physical existence so that happiness could be hidden and then found. Happiness could be given and received and then repeated all over again even better and better.

This is the beginning of the stage of existence that is known as the spiritual path. For could one simply repeat the same loving action without some improvement and be happy? For one to view progress as a path, there must be a start and way forward even if there is no end but yet another path to follow. For the following is but a scenario to be understood, for in truth it is more like an opening of a heart from one that is small and with much misunderstanding to one that is large, wise and capable of much more love. And so for there to be no misunderstanding, let us say that there is much that has to be learned, felt, incorporated and advanced in capability. In short, we grow towards God.

Now let us review yet another concept that is much misunderstood from the Cayce Readings, that of the Greater Good. For a good to be greater than all others, it must trespass the marriage of two souls who have come together to be one and in so doing create good enough for two or three or four or more. Thus, in finding that the nature of reunion is for it to multiply and to supply and nourish all who come in contact and to give no harm, there is the definition of the Greater Good: to be a lover somewhat like God Himself and to use the same methods to create good such as patience, forgiveness, grace, lightness and teaching. And so there is much to be said for the path having access to these traits both from within and without in the form of others who come to help.

Lastly there is the dictum that is nearly universal such as has come down from ancient physician oaths: Do not harm and perform much good. For no harm and much good to be performed, there is only the need to be sure that it comes from love and is returned in love. And so there is the issue of the definition of love. For love to be understood, the lover must know its origin is in pure love, for such recognition is innate in all beings. All beings respond equally well to being loved and tend to give love back, for this is the nature of the universe to be love inspired. As love lingers in one's life in the state of being given and received and returned back again, there is the sure knowledge that one is lovable, but also that one is love itself. Such love can only prosper from the center of the existence of both the giver and the receiver.

And so it is from the beginning of time that the truth has been gathered and disseminated about the giving and receiving of love. Had it not been for the lifetime of Jesus Christ, there would not have been the historical record of his life and teachings. But for these great teachers, there might have been a great loss. But those whose nature it is to publish such things, left no stone unturned to portray it clearly, so it still rings true and ever shall.

In returning to the story of the Edgar Cayce teachings, let there be no mistake that one can take the meaning to be whatever one might want to hear but yet, just like that of Christ, there is the ring of truth and the feeling of great love. And that is what draws and singes the feathers of those who would fly elsewhere in search of truth. So let's for the moment, consider how and why one might wander into the front door to find the readings so attractive. They who come in search of their own experience of God – to be loved as no other lover can do – are the seekers. So the search goes on, but yet there is another way than by searching through so many readings to find just one more inspiring moment in time when he said this or that in response to yet another request for healing. For there are many who come and go, but must find their way back again and again. For them, we would like to propose that the closeness to such a great giver is much easier than the travelogue would have it. Just go inward and reach up to the Higher Mind and let your soul peruse the psychic record until he is found. Such conversations can be profound and lasting and much good can be found and never harm.

So let's resume our search for the Higher Mind and the path to reach it. The so-called enlightenment model or even the ascension thought is nothing but the making of the Mind of God to be one's own mind. And so the concept of the cooperation between the Higher Mind and the Conscious Mind needs to be discussed. Let there be no mistake that there is no taking of free will away from anyone, nor is there any slavery of one to another, especially not to those thought to be teachers, clerics or even sisters of the garb. These have the duty and privilege to serve as role models and special delivery agents of good, but none of them are empowered to be givers of enlightenment or salvation. If just one thing would be known from these readings, it would suffice to know that there is no salvation needed, for there is no harm in the universe save in the Conscious Mind which created such a concept. Based upon fear and retribution, it has no impact whatsoever on the future of any soul except to cause it to remember itself even more fully.

So for the present moment, let's acknowledge the real truth of the matter that we are of God and that God made us to sincerely reflect himself in every manner of glory that can be. Therefore, the more that you tune into the Higher Mind and find true guidance as to how that can best be done, there is no harm and much more good. As far as we can see, there is no need for any other concept save one. By which means is one to be blessed with the accomplishment of the Highest Good, the hard way or the easy way?

First let's describe the hard way by means of the karmic reversal units at work. These are hard way advocates who like to find themselves in a real difficulty and to show themselves capable of extracting themselves in the end. Along the way there are many who have determined to be with them for various reasons and for that purpose have learned to beware of them, for there is indeed an easier way.

Let's assume that there are many along the way who say " Easy way please." For these fortunate few, there are few hardships, disasters or anything else that distracts them from their peace. Finding such to be the case, there are many who come and go looking for one to teach just such a way. Therefore, their way becomes popular and is spread around the world with great joy. On the other hand, there are those whose choice is the hard way who are making a mess of the peace lovers. For the sake of peace, there must be a way for some to be allowed to prosper and others not. And so in saying this, there is the karmic influence, which allows only good and peace to prosper and discourages the hard way by means of many bad consequences. But let us not say that one is better than the other, one is just easier and more productive of peace than the other. Both are to be tolerated, but the cards are indeed stacked in favor of the easy way as it is far more successful.

Should the wish of the group of entities who protect the earth be to dislodge the hard way followers, they can and have done so for the following of yet another grand plan. So there is no grand victory of one over the other, just the following of one way after another. Neither will one way cease to exist, because the followers of each have developed their own ways of sharing their insights. For example, should a peaceful one be abused by another, they merely need to say the words: "It is time for you to go." With these words, the other is obligated to leave them in peace. On the reverse, when one greets the other for a transaction, there are often the words: "What took you so long?" or "Where have you been?" These last words imply fault on the other and impatience and complaint and thus the interaction begins on that note and continues until one or the other leaves. The question comes up as to whether one can intend harm to another without the consent of the one to be harmed. The answer is no. It is always by mutual agreement for the furtherance of the Highest Good. And so if one is a peaceful one, there only need be made the intention of never having to suffer harm and to refuse it whenever it is offered, and so it is done.

So why would one agree to be harmed, one might ask. This is the one thing that has stumped many less evolved than the Christ Consciousness. For he alone made the distinction that no harm can come by making a transition even if it is a difficult one. For this he is named the teacher of the resurrection, although it is not of the body, but of the light body. Once the concept of the light body is well understood by the general populace, there will never again be grief at the passing of a person from one form to another. But that will be left for yet another reading. For the time being, understand that none but the body can be harmed and that it can be healed in amazing ways just by means of the proper use of the intention to do so. Without the limitation of pain, which also can be overcome by use of the intention for pain free transitioning, there is no interference for the moving from one state to another at will. But we let that be given in yet another reading.

And thus with the promise of yet many more readings of this type and better, we have begun to disclose many of the meaningful secrets of the existence of earth life. It is being given now for the use of the next thousand years of peace. For if all would but open their hearts and minds to the fact that: "It doesn't have to be so hard," then the progress of the peaceful project will enhance the earth and all of its inhabitants. We are done for now.

+

Joyce: Wow, there is a lot in this reading that I do understand, but much that I don't. Let's apply it to my life. Maybe I'll get it that way.

Peaceful One: What a fine idea. I wish that I'd thought of that. Just joking. You see that you have in fact accomplished the greatest of all accomplishments of any lifetime. You have reunited the Conscious Mind with its Soul. It is the equivalent of being in love and finding each other in the confusing crowd and coming together to be one once again. Did it fit your expectations or did you want to see the two running across a field of flowers only to fall into each other's arms?

Joyce: There you are being humorous again. I know that you do that when you are particularly happy about something. So what's up, may I ask?

Peaceful One: When you are one, you know nothing that the other does not know. You want nothing that the other does not want. You need nothing that the other cannot supply, etc. So let me want what you want. You want the joy of refusing to fear being loved and to display that the true love that you always wanted was always within yourself. Is that not true?

Joyce: Yes and no. See I can give contradictory answers as well as you. (Chuckles) Yes, I know now that no Conscious Mind can give what a Higher Mind can, so I seek answers and favors only from a Higher Mind wherever I can find it, which is everywhere.

Peaceful One: Not to say on every continent, under the deep blue sea, on the top of the highest mountain and at the bottom of the deepest valley. How am I doing?

Joyce: You are starting to sound like me when I want to write poetry and I am starting to sound like you when you want to be serious about explaining something. Which is which?

Peaceful One: That's the point, after all.

Joyce: Of course, we are becoming one as we are with all others and it doesn't matter the appearances in the physical plane.

Peaceful One: How wise you are to forestall any grief of any kind with any of your companions of peace. And yet another reading of grace is on its way. It is for both you and your readers to understand how the growth of one soul through its life path toward reunion is also the purpose of the earth's incarnation as a beautiful blue planet.

A Reading

Topic Reading: Life Plans and Spiritual Growth 5.25.12
Peace and Light Association
Peaceandlight01@aol.com

A life plan is just what it seems to be. Before each incarnation, the opportunity arises for souls desiring to experience themselves as God givers in the realm of the physical plane known as earth to form a plan for that experience. In this thought process, there are many considerations to be made. Should one just continue the concerns of the prior life or insert oneself into yet another arena of concern? Does one have the support and strength to endure and perfect the goal? Should one alter one's physical form to suit the conditions of the plan? Who will be the willing compatriots? How will the sequence of events be ordered so that no experience is lost and all can be gained? For this all to be done correctly, there is a need for a forecaster of sorts whose job it is to be informed of every possible outcome so that all experiences can be evaluated and given the best use. This forecaster is none other than the Christ Consciousness, for he alone has the power and responsibility to organize and empower the earth experiences for only the Highest Good. With this in place, there is the sealing of the pact for one to contact the other for help. No concern is left undecided. For all souls to be given such a precise plan, one might think that all has been ordained, but such is not the case. More there is one and then the other choice and with the bending of the will to better and better exemplify the will of God for peace and good will, then the new choices are brought forth. The best analogy would be the modern video games that offer first one choice and an outcome and then another. It is indeed a complex program.

Once these choices have been laid out and the soul is duly prepared with the agenda being placed in its unconscious memory, then the pulling of the ripcord takes place. We use this analogy for it is indeed a falling from a high state to a much lower one. As one of the fine-feathered friends might say: "Come fly with me." For there are many who have come and gone who stay behind for the use and assistance of the beloved one participating in the experience. Never let it be misunderstood, one does not take one's entire soul from one state to another, just a small part of it, much like a child who spends some time day dreaming but the most of it elsewhere.

Thus in finding that there is little falling, but actually closing down the portals of grand communication with all beings everywhere and all that they know and can do, the task of the lifetime becomes to open once again to that which the soul once had. And with this understanding, there is little left to understand but the finding out as to how and why one would shut down something so fine as a soul mind into such a limited space as a Conscious Mind. For that to be so, there must be a great deal of good to be gained and for this to be understood, let us expound for a moment on the necessity for joy.

In the universe, there is a river of energy that flows from the source of all energy and back again, finding itself a deeper level. Abounding with joy is essentially the experience of being in the deepest channel of that river. Let's take this analogy in parts the same as we did that of the baby. As a river flows, it picks up more and more energy as it descends even an inch, carrying with it all that is in its path or rides upon its surface. Thus we find that there is no analogy left better than to be carried upon this river of energy back to one's home or source. Once found, the deepest channel runs the fastest and truest and so it is easy to just sit in a boat and let it carry you. Neither are there shoals nor rocks nor eddies in the deep channel. In order to attain such a presence in the channel, one must dedicate one's life to the seeking of the Highest Good in all situations. It is easy to be prosperous, healthy, happy and profoundly well occupied once one achieves this channel. But where is it to be found? It seems to be guarded by the shallows alive with alligators, rocks and eddies that turn one in circles. It is with one or the other of the great tools that are being offered here that one can find one's way back to the central channel and busily count one's blessings.

For this to happen in one's life there must be the understanding that there are no circumstances that are too hard or unforgiving to endure with patience. For with such determination, one might persevere in patience through a divorce, an illness, rejection by others, a financial downturn, etc. Much like the story of Job in the Bible, there are those who would tempt him to curse the maker of these circumstances, but later Job just laughs as he says that the same God brought him wealth, grace and acclaim as brought him poverty and shame, so why should he discard any of these experiences? With this firmly in mind, he knows from whence he came and his life path decisions are all essentially the same: turn to God with thanks at every turn of events without blame to himself or anyone else, including God.

From whence and why would such experiences be given, one might ask? The whys and wherefores have more to do with the current state of affairs within the neighborhood of the mind than with physical reality. For if the mind can remain at peace in circumstances of deprivation, then it can also remain at peace in plenty. For one is just more of the good than the other. In the story of Job, as long as Job was alive, he knew that God blessed him.

So with this firmly in mind, there is yet another Long Story to be told. For this story to be told, it must be admitted that none are much longer than an hour in length to tell, but eons of time to form and to live, so the topic of time must be broached. For time to begin and end with a specific event, there must be the intention to be given for the accomplishment of one or another thing to be or to do. For this to be said with authority, it must be shown that there is never an event in time and in space to be had without the intention for peace, for peace consciousness is the parcel of land upon which one can stand forever and never be disturbed or challenged.

And so we find that those whose wish it is to accomplish things in time and space in peace have the duty to endure the passage of time and the denial of much that is immediate in other times, but in some times virtually non-existent. For these times to be understood, let's simply call them the doldrums or slack times. The purpose of these times is to expand a mind through the denial of one thing or another and, with the stretching of the mind and the heart, there is much to be gained. For in gaining the high ground or the deep channel so to speak, all else can be had freely and in great accord with the will for the Highest Good. And once something is had by this method, there is never again doubt that it came from somewhere else and was graciously given, and thus love is felt with its companion, joy.

And as the joy is felt, there is the desire for more and more and so forth. So from such small beginnings of just a little bit of time spent in front of a sunny window, so much good has been attained that time will never be viewed in the same way and good will never be regarded as luck, but rather as the raft sailing along upon its own back. That the soul is the source of all good in one's life is no doubt. And so the long story starts all over again for how could it be that the great soul that one is could ever forsake its small fry?

And now we come once again to the taking of a short intermission so as to refresh the soul, body and mind of this one with a short dialogue. Amen.

+

Joyce: Would you give me an example of something in my life that illustrates my life path?

Peaceful One: With whom are you speaking right now, my dear one, that you cannot see me within all of the experiences of your life? It was me all of the time. I was calling the shots for every experience and forming every intention. I was putting you through the paces, so to speak, so that we could grow up together in peace, nothing else.

Joyce: What? Are you saying that you are completely running my life, excuse me, our life? Everything that happens is made to be that way on purpose from your point of view, not mine?

Peaceful One: Exactly. I've been unmasked.

Joyce: So you sent both husbands to me?

Peaceful One: My compatriots and I were those husbands.

Joyce: Good grief! Then you gave me both the disappointing marriages and the sunny window and the messages for a reason?

Peaceful One: Precisely.

Joyce: Hold on here, you are bridging the gap between the dimensions or some such thing. If I now know this, then. . . . . .then, what?

Peaceful One: Then we can play in peace for you know where your life came from, what it is all about and how it will progress.

Joyce: Well then what's the point?

Peaceful One: Don't you like to play with life? Don't you like to create new and interesting experiences and see where they lead? Where's your sense of adventure?

Joyce: Oh, I give up. You are impossible today. I don't know what just happened, but I have definitely lost my mind.

Peaceful One: Which one?

Joyce: Ok, you can stop now. I need a nap.

Peaceful One: Ok, if you want to, but I'm there, too.

Joyce: Sigh.

Peaceful One: SIGH!

Chapter Seven: Trusting the Highest Good

It was not a good day or a bad day, but certainly a beautiful day when I set out to go to work. I had plenty of time, the sun was shining and I was listening to great, peaceful music. As I drove down a road, another car pulled out in front of me at the last minute and I helplessly slammed into the side of it, wrecking my car. Fortunately, neither of us was injured. She said that she didn't see me, so she had no bad intention, possibly only inattention.

When I arrived home and rested for the night, I was interested in talking to the Peaceful One about this experience for I have been driving fifty years without an accident, and it was astounding to me that this happened. I had gotten over being afraid, but I guess I was a bit mad and didn't understand how this could even happen to me.

+

Joyce: OK, you have a lot of explaining to do. Yesterday I was in a car wreck that should have been fatal, but I walked away without a scratch. What were you thinking? I thought that we were leading our life together and that I was protected by the intention for the Highest Good. What do you have to say?

Peaceful One: OK, you say one thing and then another. How could I have subjected you to such an experience and have you write another book about the life path phenomenon so that all can come to know and appreciate how their life experiences come to be? Then you say why not just kill me whenever you want? We cannot take this line of thought too far, for even you have discarded it, so for now, let's admit that there are indeed three of us at work here. Conscious Mind, Higher Mind and the third one is Me, the Light Enforcer, the Giver of Life itself, God and his extension agent, Christ Consciousness.

Joyce: Yes, I have been running through many explanations of the event and none of them seem to fit the intention for the Highest Good. Maybe it is more complex than the Conscious Mind knows. I'll bet you have a good reading in store for Dear Reader and me. Dear Reader makes four; you know how dearly I love them all.

Peaceful One: Well, then that makes a lot of us all, for all were on target for this experience to happen. Perhaps you wondered why the medic called you stubborn for refusing to go to the hospital. Why did he choose that word when you were told in the next hour that the purpose of the event was to convince you of what you were told long ago but you stubbornly refused to believe? Your purpose in life is to be a conveyer of the Highest Good teaching and not much else, so therefore, there is no purpose in your portraying yourself with fear of anything, certainly not going out to do your work. Therefore, we have stumbled across or maybe better yet crashed into the first topic of the chapter: The Soul's Path.

Joyce: I'm smiling to think that my purpose in this life is so clear. As I look back at my life, I see so many things that were in preparation for the task, but I've always had good luck and even in 50 years of driving, never had an accident, so how was this accident part of my path?

Peaceful One: More a correction for better acknowledgement of the truth of the engagement, so to speak, which is better said to be that of a warrior for peaceful thoughts in all cases. So let's see how that works for you to be seen as an older lady who lightly gets out of her car after a usually fatal car wreck, refuses a trip to the hospital and demands to be picked up and taken home then the next day she goes out and buys herself a steak dinner for the nourishment needed to repair the little damage that was done. I might add that this was all done with precise instructions from the highest sources and then some. How did it work for you?

Joyce: Well, it was really scary, but actually I was more upset about missing work where I teach supervisors how to treat employees in a peaceful and effective manner.

But back to your line of thought. What does that say about me and my purpose? Is that where you are leading?

Peaceful One: How well put could that be? Let's assume for one moment that I am not afraid of anything and yet I go to the museum of dark places and see lots of supposedly dangerous and frightful things, however, I come out laughing as to the extent of the effort made to present something that is so unnecessary, namely fear.

Joyce: So it's not so much courage, boldness, timidity or strength as it is veracity? I'm to tell the truth about fear in general and then others can apply it to their own particular situations?

Peaceful One: Exactly. And how perfect is it that you have come to be moved from one lane of traffic to another with so little damage even when you felt some fear? Is it indeed just the thinking of a thought that makes for an event to happen or is it the making of an intention and then sticking to it that creates events in order and alignment of all good things needed to accomplish the purpose of a lifetime?

Joyce: I don't know, you tell me. OK, I have to stop here because I can't say things like that anymore. After all, you and I are not separate and we can't count one, two, three or more. In fact, I suppose we will have to stop calling ourselves you and me and chose another name that reflects our oneness.

Peaceful One: If the reader will remember that we are more complex than two individuals having a conversation and admit that we should be called thousands engaging in the same quest, then we can continue to use our current names. Indeed, the process of incarnation into a Conscious Mind is a confusing experience for all who undertake it and it is not named properly.

Joyce: I'd be sure to be compassionate with the ones who are still confused, for I am surely one of them myself. OK, so what name could we call ourselves, meaning the thousands engaging in the same quest?

Peaceful One: How about the Companions for Peaceful Living? Or CPL for short. We would all be one under that intention for it is a purposeful thing, not just an affiliation of a few who like each other for a time.

Joyce: And we are all part of the Great Oneness, some incarnated and some not, right?

Peaceful One: Yes. We are all bonded together under one leadership, which is the Christ Consciousness who is so bonded to his Father that they can only be called One.

Joyce: So sometimes you speak as the Christ Consciousness because you are at one with that leadership, which is at one with the Godhead itself? Pretty good resume, I'd think.

Peaceful One: Indeed. Now we come to the most urgent need and your latest sense of adventure. How are you going to get your car fixed and all that is amiss back into order while you are sitting here working on this dialogue with us?

Joyce: Well, that's a good question. I'd say that I should take a break and make the necessary calls and get started on the day's activities, but are you saying something different?

Peaceful One: How could we be CPL if not all in cooperation? So many have already been calling and making arrangements on your behalf just because you signed up to be the Lord of the Rings of Peace, so to speak.

Joyce: So all was put in place long ago in the whole system of insurance and accident investigations and I will be given all that I need to get back behind the wheel?

Peaceful One: Yes, indeed it is so. Do you now accept and believe that all is in order even in the case of a serious accident?

Joyce: Yes, I do.

Peaceful One: Then go ahead and order your day for the good of the whole, which is your goal, your support, your truth and the way that you will be living the rest of your many lives. No more or no less.

Several hours later.

Joyce: Things are progressing nicely and yes, I can identify those who are helping me have the intention for the Highest Good. Once one learns to look for it, the difference is easy to see. Also, I find that it is much more abundant than I thought that it would be. There are many who have also had accidents and come forward with compassion to be kind to me for they see themselves in the same situation and want to heal their own memories by helping me. That is a beautiful thing about people, even those who work the lowliest jobs or do the most distasteful and difficult tasks in our society, like EMR crews, police officers, clerks, janitors, customer service operators and truck drivers.

Peaceful One: Once one can identify who is who, then there is the need to see that they are all you facing the same emergency. That is oneness for sure. Now whom do we call ourselves who help each other through emergency situations?

Joyce: They are the Compassionate Helpers.

Peaceful One: Well then they are all linked together because the word for compassion is love and so is the word for peace, love. Therefore they are all part of the Christ Consciousness at work in everyday life spreading their twin wings of grief relief and pain removal. Such healing was depicted on the tomb walls in Egypt as twin wings spread open. Once one has this twin experience, then one is capable of taking off for parts unknown, knowing that the destination is made of love.

Joyce: I've seen these two wings in photos and I always thought that they were beautiful, like eagle wings, large and strong and capable of soaring for a long time with little effort. Are you saying that they were a symbol of needing help and then turning around and giving help?

Peaceful One: How wise you are. How could you have asked the brother turtle to stand on his tail and show you the moon and the sun on his belly in order to show you the way home? These are the images of the Indians of another time and place who understood that the objects in the sky and the elements of the earth are indeed the seed of compassion come to call.

Joyce: What do you mean compassion come to call? This is interesting. I want to know more.

Peaceful One: How could we have given you more to look after unless you had first looked after your own needs as a being of grace? Thus those who call themselves gatherers of moonbeams were calling themselves needy of the compassion and peace of a winter's night with a high moon, and those who needed the healing and strength of the sun did so as well. Thus we find that each civilization had its calling for things for different reasons and some told of high favor standing in line at church while others told of simple huts on the forest floor. No matter the circumstances or buildings, the moon and the sun have something to say about how we live each day.

Joyce: This is fascinating because, as I was coming home late last night from the incident, the moon was large, bright and gleaming with shimmering colors. Are you saying that the incident purposefully happened on the night of a full moon for a reason? What was that reason?

Peaceful One: What one could have seen if they had ethereal vision was a long stream of light beams coming and going from the earth as many who were dreaming of better things were asking for relief from their grief and suffering. Others who were streaming their gratitude for having been given relief, were giving strength to those needing it. So there is no need to know where the Christ Consciousness resides, it resides in the minds, hearts and deeds of those who come in peace, giving compassion and those who are grateful for it. If not one, then all can be called by the same name. Thus there is no need to be in compassion or grief, just send gratitude and appreciation so that another can catch it and find it good and then relay it on to another.

Joyce: So I was receiving healing relief from others when I looked at the moon and when I give thanks, I give it on to anyone else who needs it. So are full moon times better than others for this phenomenon?

Peaceful One: That is so, as many civilizations well understood. Therefore many a ceremony of healing was conducted under such understanding and much grief was relieved.

Joyce: I am remembering my science now. The moon only reflects light from the sun and is at times shadowed by the earth based on its rotation, but only one side receives light, the other is always dark. What is its function?

Peaceful One: Once one has an understanding of how light works as an instrument of Higher Being, sending and receiving energy, it is clear that the two sides create an energy flow that is particularly strong when full light is on one side and not on the other. Thus the energy establishes itself because it is both light and dark, not just because light is good and dark is bad, but because the ratio of difference is so strong that a flow is created. Within this flow there is the need to be seen as an alternating current, thus there is a shimmering effect as much is stirred up, shared and energized because of the need and the filling of the need. It is much like receptivity and giving between the genders. Much that is good is created. Thus the purpose of experiences on the earth to be in need is indeed to be the generators of much giving and thus much good. For we who have come for this great energy flow are filled with wonder at how well it works and wish that it would continue forever. Thus we have willed that, for the time being, that too much greed or need-creating cease so that the balance can be reestablished by more giving. Thus we come to the main topic of our conversation. How can the soul's life path on this earth be understood?

Joyce: I just love it how you talk about one thing and illustrate a principle and then show the same principle at work in another instance. It gives the impression that there is great unity in the natural and spiritual worlds.

Peaceful One: That is so. The saying that light is love is just such an example. If one has compassion for one in need following an emergency and offers help, then the light bulb is lit for a transmission of the heart. Once a heart is open to giving, which often happens as a result of forgiveness and the offering of help, then it is capable of generating much electricity of love. Once generation starts, there is no end and those who are so dear to you as readers of your books are absorbing this at this very moment and are wondering how their love for each other can be so powerful.

Joyce: So we have love, light, electricity and probably some others which are energy flows operating on the principle of the giving and receiving principle. Are they all the same energy only in different forms or for different uses?

Peaceful One: Well said, but just one more fact to entertain. How come, as you are fond of saying, does one form of energy come from one's heart chakra which is spiral in nature and the others come from a spiraling vortex of the sun and yet another from a wire wound around a piece of metal?

Joyce: Well, I remember that you said that one direction of a spiral is outgoing and the other ingoing, so I guess that means that the heart, the sun and a piece of wire and metal are capable of setting a direction.

Peaceful One: Yes, and wouldn't that amount to the phenomenon of setting an intention with one's mind?

Joyce: Oh, my goodness. Now I see how important one's intention is. It literally commands huge energy forces of the universe. Wow and wow again.

Peaceful One: When one sets an intention to be in need such as the need to purchase a car, then one creates a circular pendulum flow that is circular to the left which draws inward what forces of nature can address that need appropriately and once it is satisfied, then the field is reversed, creating an out flow of satisfaction of the need. Once this is understood, the flows of emotion can be viewed as just such an emotional intention. For if one feels like a victim or in need of protection, then the protection is drawn to fill that need whether it be adding more weight or being given a key to lock a door from an intruder, or something so simple as a friend to call. When the need is fully filled, then the reverse happens and one intends to help others who have the same need. Thus much more good is given than was received, for one might have the need once and devote the rest of one's life to giving to that need in others. Thus the intention for the Highest Good is replete with the intention of relief of grief and the counterbalancing healing as a result of help, thus the two wings of a bird well balanced lead to flight carrying one well above the plane of understanding. This is essentially the purpose of a soul's choice to be in suffering and then to experience compassion and to give service to others who have also suffered.

Joyce: That is a very big thought. I'll bet that is the meaning of the law of attraction. Tell me more.

Peaceful One: Well dear one, you have graced me with receiving these transmissions and so in grace I have been giving you much grace of self-healing. There will be no bruises or even a scrape. Neither will there be any soreness of muscles or any adjustment to the spine needed, for all is well with thee because we are three, Christ Consciousness, me and thee and we all work for the same cause and this causes us to relieve each other and to be at peace. At the same time, there are those listening to this reading wondering how they can also be three and so we allow for them to come into this reading and ask their own questions.

Joyce: OK???

Peaceful One: If you will allow me, let the one who allows that she can be a radio show host for a call in show on these topics be the one to invite others to come and go as they need. Being in need of a career in which she is heard, we have provided her with the relief of this need and since the callers will be in need of being heard and answered, much energy will be released and those doing both will be calling themselves a new name such as the Companions for Peaceful Living and much more good will be done. For now we are done, for you are in need of a rest and a peaceful meal of great strength and so it will be given to you. We rest in peace. Amen.

3.28.13 Continuation of Car Wreck

Joyce: After a good nights sleep, I am up, cleaning house and working on ordering my life to do the role of Teacher of the Highest Good. I feel no muscle soreness; I have no bruises or injuries of any kind even after a 30MPH head-on collision into a SUV. I know that I was protected and blessed and that I will have another beautiful new car that will serve me and my purposes very well.

Dear Reader, to be honest, it was quite an experience in learning to trust both my guidance and the loving care with which I am given experiences in my life. At one point, I realized that my soul could take me out of this lifetime whenever it wanted, for whatever purpose, and my Conscious Mind would be powerless to stop it, so I had to inquire as to how these decisions are made. It was, however, a very complex subject. The short answer is that each soul has a life purpose and both minds cooperate to achieve that and when it is done, then a pre-planned transition takes place. The long answer had to do with fears creating fearful experiences and how the earth was designed to be a reflection of the Nature of God. I would suggest that you not draw any firm conclusions just yet and let the dialogues progress a while longer. These higher understandings take many steps to begin to understand and with each step there is a healing of fear, so it is wise to enjoy each step and be in no hurry.

With that said, I'd also say that you have to be part of the Highest Good companionship to have continued to read this far. I imagine you to be like Bastion in *The Neverending Story* who reads a book for enjoyment, but finds that he becomes the main character in the book. He accepted the challenge to give the empress a new name, his mother's name. With that he was healed of his grief over her death and found that she lived as the empress of his heart forever, even though he proceeded in life with his feet on the ground. So welcome to this, the story of your own existence and if you have opened up to your own channel between your two minds, do keep your own journal and ask your own questions. You will always be happy, healed, cared for, blessed and never frightened or harmed. For me, I will press on with yesterday's questions. I hope that I am asking the same questions that you want to know about as well. Here goes!

Joyce: Dearest Peaceful One, we greet each other again.

Peaceful One: Where did you go that I was not there?

Joyce: Point taken.

Peaceful One: I was in the car wreck shouting "NO" all of the way into the black SUV. I was in the ambulance telling them that I did not want to go to the hospital as I had my own guidance as to what to do next. I was on the phone asking for Jim to come and pick me up and to cancel my work for the week. I came home and felt grateful to be safe at home and to soak in a hot tub of Epsom salts and to rest at peace in my own bed. I called the insurance agent and I was she who took over your case and made it progress much faster than you might imagine. I have been the friends and family who have been expressing how much you mean to them and that if you had exited their lives, that they would sorely miss you. I have been channeling information about the others who are about to meet you once again to form new friendships and relationships, so they can be known in the way that fosters the best unions. Shall I go on?

Joyce: Actually yes, it is very comforting to hear over and over again how we are all one. So I have to ask, whose decision would it be for me to transition out of this life?

Peaceful One: Both of us. We planned it long ago. Nothing is programmed into your experience except what facilitates the life purpose and yours is to be a long-lived teacher and explainer of the Highest Good including technology issues. So, my dear, you are fated to live a long and rich life without undue trouble or grief except what you create for yourself. This experience was of the nature of a surprise so that you can cast yourself easily into each and every experience without fear and enjoy what comes next.

You did admirably well, I might add. Did you notice that your heart rate and blood pressure was not above normal when they took the measurements and that you were fully conscious and alert at all times except for the moment of impact. We shut off the brain for an instant so that you would not hear the crunch as you had asked not to remember the sound. Then we turned it on once again so you could function as planned. You are neither a victim nor a pawn of a higher power. You are the willing cooperator in a grand plan for all to be aware of the nature of the Highest Good at work in creation.

Joyce: Oh! For the sake of my Dear Readers, how will they know their purpose so they can know of their life path?

Peaceful One: How can one search for anything? Just by opening to channel, one can learn their own life path and their purpose in life. It will be a gradual leading thing, for there are many things to explain before it can be put before them plainly, but those who persevere will be given what they need to accomplish their plan for it is in the Highest Good to do so. So what is your plan for the day?

Joyce: Well, I cleaned house and am doing this reading, but it is a nice day, so I might take a walk. My farm helper is coming so I will talk to him about the care of the farm. I'm packing a bag to be at my daughter's house as she is about to deliver her second child and I will be there to assist her. What's your plan for the day?

Peaceful One: Much the same as yours so we are at peace for now. If you would energize nothing more than this, you would be perfectly happy and at peace and all else would be delivered to you, including a load of wood and a beautiful baby. We are masters of not wanting demise and, knowing how you are about expectations and anticipations, we have a pre-arranged agreement to be in attendance as things develop but not to give you predictions as such, other than general arrangements that can be altered as we go. We do this to assure you of what is in the works so to speak, but not alert you to any action other than what is obvious for you to do today or tomorrow, etc. Do we understand each other now?

Joyce: Yes, I understand that I have the habit of anticipating things and forming judgments about them and using that to change things for today that do not need to be changed, just because I think that something else might happen. It is very stressful for me and keeps me in fear and regret. So thanks, my friends and family are always cautioning me about this.

Peaceful One: But that does not mean that we are mean to you and withdraw what has been promised or prohibit you from having what you want and need, especially if it is for the PURPOSE. Indeed, these are the experiences that are speeded up and will arrive in a surprise nature just like the accident. Are we agreed about that?

Joyce: Yes, we are agreed. I like making these agreements open and mutually conscious. I don't like how the Conscious Mind cannot know and has to go in the dark, so to speak. It fosters fear.

Peaceful One: Precisely. Why do you think that you feel so strongly about every reader opening their minds to their own channel so all can live powerful and happy lives in open communication and cooperation? That is the grand design, by the way, and you are cooperating to make that obvious.

Joyce: Precisely! I got that. Gee, I'm getting smarter the longer I talk to you. (Chuckle) I guess we are both the teacher and the student.

Peaceful One: Well, smartee, let's get back to the discussion of yesterday. You were interested in the moon's reflection of the heart energies of the population of the earth, receiving needs and giving out joy. What about the sun, you were going to ask?

Joyce: Yes, I was. The sun is the source of the light and heat energy of our solar system. What is its function in regard to the rivers of energy that flow through the universe?

Peaceful One: Well put. What a good student you are. You will be a graceful teacher, I might add. Yes, the sun is the inventor of all life upon the earth and all other planets in this system. It sends an unlimited supply of the energy, grace and nutrients that are needed to sustain life on earth, therefore, we would define it as the local source of the life stream given by God. There are other stars for other systems, but in this life stream, there are many more resources than is commonly known. Besides radiant heat, light, ultrasonic and radio transmissions called static, there are many other radiations. As one would see in the glare of the sun on a hot road, it has a shimmering nature much like we noted with the moon. So all radiations from the sun are spiral or circular and participate in the unique qualities of that shape. The round shape has the nature of having no exit points and all is contained within it. For this reason, we are content within it and so it was the shape chosen for many temples and ceremonial sites.

It is only in defining the shape of a place that one can know what went on there. For the square places sent energy to four points and then continued around such as the pyramid, the stone foundations of rectangular structures were similar. Their plan was to spend more time and energy on two longer sides than on the shorter two. The square has the function of the four points to be seen and appreciated and not much more. With the octagon shape, there is the need to appreciate the eight-sided figure for what it is, a prison of no return from the defeat of one direction only to be turned to another and another until one returns once again to the beginning.

Thus, the one original shape that is peaceful is the circle and thus the sun's rays emanate from an orb spiral downward to the earth in expanding circles called spirals for the purpose of not losing much and sending more for a long time. Thus the intention for the sun is to be a long lasting source of God's love and grace which will never diminish until the core of its energy is used up and not before. For nothing can disturb it and it needs no protection and its radiance can be seen from all parts of space for billions of miles in all directions. Thus, it was used as a universal symbol for God. With its emissions thoroughly understood and unraveled, so to speak, there is the possibility that all who came to live upon this earth can feed, house and warm themselves in a university of peace. For the sun is as much a teaching tool about the nature of God as it is a fiery furnace of heat and light. Thus it can be said that the sun is the giver of gifts such as was depicted by the drawings of Akhenaton and his wife who sit facing each other with the sun in between. Each ray is giving a different gift symbolized by the little hands, which they are obliged to interpret and to receive on behalf of their people.

From this position in the sun disk scene, there is much peace to be had, for none would be a pleasure for another if their intention were not peaceful, thus they both touch the rays and smile. Secondly, their hands are cupped upward in reception of the grace in the same gesture as the cupped hands from the rays. It is this mutual reception that makes for the partnerships that are so valid in life, much like we just did when we agreed how your readings would occur in regard to the near future events. Once a mating of the twin engines of fate: giving and receiving, has occurred, then there is no reason not to spawn new life in the form of children or grain or the richness of a new invention of peaceful revolution. Thus we find that many who have come this far are opened to the need to be in touch with the radiant ones of peace, the Hathors. Thus we will alert the reader to expect further discussion from them to a later time when more information has arrived and there is a receptive environment.

For now, just let us begin once again to know and to love the beatitude of the blessed ones: Those whose peace surpasses the understanding of the Conscious Mind, which means to be in cooperation with their Higher Mind, will be at peace forever, for they and their kind will inherit the earth in peace.

Joyce: Thank you, I know that this long and generous reading will spark many more, but for now, I sense that what was given needs to be understood and accepted before much more can be given. I am at rest. Peace be with you.

Attending to Relationship with Spirit

Peaceful One: What shall we dialogue about today? Why are you not asking this question as you usually do?

Joyce: I'm thinking about your comment that the accident was a course correction. I'm thinking: "How was I not paying attention to you that I needed a car crash to get my attention?" This thought makes me sad, as I love talking to you so and this statement implies that I not paying attention to you. Did you need to do this because I was errant in some way?

Peaceful One: What one thing did I say that lead you to believe that you were errant?

Joyce: You said course correction and that I was stubborn. It reminds me of when I was told as a child that I was too proud. I was very hurt because I thought that I was just being me and that it was OK for me to do that. The message of the correction was that me being me was not OK.

Peaceful One: How about we take the time to get a true recognition of what the event was all about. For suddenly your heart is sending me a true signal of what it wants: a truly gentle and kind relationship with me and all others without undue surprises or knocks on the head.

Joyce: Yes, that's it. If you caused the crash, then deep inside I cannot trust that our relationship is gentle and kind. Also, the other party was not aware of others as she pulled out. If I had been harmed, then all who could be helped by me and my work would have been harmed as well.

Peaceful One: Well, then, dear one, what about your kindness to yourself in giving yourself to service in complete trust that your compassion to yourself and all others would rise to the surface in this writing. Would that all come to the realization that driving skills are in great need of revision if they truly want to be citizens in a peaceful world.

Joyce: You mean that I had the experience just so I would pray that no one ever again would suffer a car crash and write about it to raise awareness of how attentive driving leads to peace?

Peaceful One: What more could have been said about you than that the compassion of one and the other could come together in this book to encourage all who have experienced an ill fated trip to be careful to ask for the Highest Good in all kinds of ways and thus the consciousness of peace and property would be enhanced.

Joyce: So you are saying that each of us should set the intention for the Highest Good before we get behind the wheel and do all that we can to assure our safety and attentiveness while driving because we are engaging in a relationship of peace on the road. That's an awesome thought. That means that each time that we set this intention and each time we drive somewhere, that we are expanding peace upon the earth and engaging in a loving relationship with all others that we meet on the road.

Peaceful One: How awesome is that? Did not Christ say: "Go with peace."

Joyce: They didn't have cars in those days, but the direction still holds true. I like this a lot. It has an intention for peace and the method is peaceful. Sorry I had to go through this experience, but I see the good that has been given as a result.

Peaceful One: Just the same for the escaped mules. Now that the phenomena of animals has been explained and compassion for both the human and the animal has been elicited, there will be no more finding of reason to not accept meat when needed nor to waste it on an everyday meals of great proportions. All will be peaceful. It will allow people who make decisions about animals to be guided by peaceful thought processes. No harm will come and much good will result. In short, the Highest Good is the outcome. Well done good and faithful servant of the Highest Good.

Joyce: Yeah! I got it. I'll take that accolade and wear it proudly; after all, I gave my beautiful red car to earn it.

Peaceful One: And then some. You also gave up your habit of stubbornly thinking that you are at fault or that anything bad could come to you by your just being you. No more or less would have been a good outcome, but so much more was intended, so much was given. Did you hear me talking to you all of the time through this experience?

Joyce: Yes, but it took me awhile to put it all together in the best understanding. I guess that was the course correction. You were patient and kind to me until I got it right and all of the time, I suffered no pain and much gain. The Highest Good was given to me as it is to all participants.

Peaceful One: How right you are right here and right now. There's not so much the progress or the education, just the discovery of an open heart ready to receive you at all times and In all conditions. Nothing but peace, my dearest, nothing but peace. Now let's not ever have anything between us again that can't be solved by a few references to our being one.

For it is a gift of a great being who came to be present this weekend of Easter (Christ Consciousness) and, in finding that none but the finest of his followers is yet trying to get his message across to so many that she lay awake at night and nearly all day writing and rewriting in an engaging way, to say that you are me and we three are all the same as all other threesomes.

Joyce: The threesome that you are referring to is you, me and any other one that I am engaging with. Right?

Peaceful One: Yes, unless you'd like to include all four of us: two Conscious Minds and two Higher Minds. With three of us, it makes six. And with that there is much fun to be had, for it is in the letting loose of the long held pain and misery of thinking that you could ever be separate or bad, that the joy of the reality of nature can be enjoyed.

Joyce: Oh, that feels so good. So what is the reality of nature?

Peaceful One: I thought that you would never ask, for I have been sitting here for so long looking out in the green pasture wondering about the clouds moving about, the birds singing and the plants growing. How do they know what to do and what do they give to me as an individual that is meaningful?

Joyce: I thought that you would never ask is not the way to ask one who loves you so. Just kidding. How have I been missing this?

Peaceful One: You have not been missing a bit of this. The Conscious Mind has been so preoccupied with time and space matters that other openings to our heart have been enjoyed, but not consciously so.

Joyce: Oh, you are talking about mental preoccupation with thoughts, plans, expectations, judgments, etc. So you are saying to relax these things further so that the natural world can speak to me and I can enjoy them. Is that right?

Peaceful One: Not that it's right or wrong; just that it is an example of how this whole thing works. For how could the grace of a blade of grass be any different that the stroke of a pen? How could the flight of a dove through air be any different than the turning of a wheel on pavement? In some ways nature is more reliable because it has no Conscious Mind intervention unless you insert it to be so. But be it so close to everyone's existence and even survival, the air, water, earth and fire are the four elements of earth's existence that can be tallied as the four states of mental existence as well.

Joyce: That was a sudden turn. I feel that you are giving a great teaching again.

Peaceful One: Once again is not again. It has been an ongoing thing for all eons of time upon the earth. How does the air bend around a thing or push against a rock with force? Does it not know its direction of choice and does it not pursue it with determination and gain energy as it interacts with other substances? This is just the same with our relationships in life. We set out in attendance to one thing or another and encounter either a resistance or a support of our own force. For when do we get angry and rebel most? Is it not when we are resisted or rebuffed? And so do we move in the direction that has least resistance until we make it around the object and find ourselves on the other side without resistance and in fact with a vacuum, which carries us, further onward? Thus it is that none who have come to you can stay very long, for their resistance is of the kind that cannot make peace with the kind one that you convey. But upon their return, there will be no mistaking the participation at such a level as to never have to say I'm sorry again.

So let's return once again to the discussion of the peace process as it affects nature. Is not the fire one that both consumes and transforms one substance into another so neither can be contained in the flames, only transformed by them? In fact, the flames are of no consequence, for if nothing is given to feed them, then they vanish. And is that not the making of an intention for peace to prevail upon the earth and none else? If little fear is offered to be consumed and transformed, then the flame vanishes. But when more is brought, then more is sought for the transformation. Thus we find that none who have been informed of their heritage have yet given much to the flames, but you have indeed given the spark which can be used over and over again to grant the leaving of pain and suffering and the entering into joy.

And leave us not in pain and suffering is also the wish to be cleansed, nurtured and not irritated with sin and grief, so do we not plunge ourselves into the pool of water that is grief relief and arise without any stain, save what we have named to be our own. And in doing so, do we not moisturize and rub our skin so that new growth and the ability to touch and feel each other in compassion result? Thus it is the sin of nervous conviction that all is not in peace that we have allowed to be given away for a new awareness that not ever means not ever. For you are indeed a protected one and will remain so in peace forever. So amen to that.

Lastly we have the ground and the earth, which rises to support us, giving food and drink to be available to us when we need it. For its support is as high as the highest mountaintop to the deepest trench of the ocean floor. And so it has come to pass that there are walkers upon every piece of ground. As well even the glass made from sand is alerted that the trails of memories that lay upon the earth are so many and so varied that there are no places without the peace of the peace bringers. Thus you are directed to travel in peace for peace has been brought wherever you go. Travel through the long held beliefs of families, tribes, communities and religions, to the simple passing of a beast or a bird or insect. So let us inspect the fear of the land and dismiss it at last. For where does the sun rise, but always in the East and where does it set, but always in the West? And where do the clouds form, but in the sky and nowhere else.

And so it has been just for this that we have traveled so far just to understand the poem that was given at the beginning of the book. My dearest, you are loved by the sun, the wind, the rain, the moon, the earth and the fire, for they come and they go just to make a way for you. For they declare peace to be their reason and purpose. Thus in finding that just one more moment in time can be taken in this time and place, that much that was started is both never completed, and at the same time always accomplished. Starting right now, "Go with Peace and attend to the spirit of peace for there is nowhere else to go on this earth. For it is a consecrated place and peace resides within every rock, stream, field and hollow."

For my heart does not need to choose to always be open to you. Indeed, it is so big that, in fact, you, all of you without exception, are already living within it.

Easter Sunday, 2013

The End of Volume Two

Forward to Volume Three

Peaceful One: "Sorry to be such a basket case for so long a time, " you are thinking this about Volume One and Two are you not? Where was my sense of humor?

Joyce: Yes, I can finally see that not only was everything OK, but it was even marvelously joyful.

Peaceful One: Do you notice that now I am leading you and you are just responding? It used to be the other way, you know.

Joyce: How did that happen?

Peaceful One: Which one is the right one to lead? Is that what you are wondering about?

Joyce: How come you don't answer what I ask? You answer what I mean to ask.

Peaceful One: How come you don't say what you mean? By the way, why do you say "How come?"

Joyce: See, you said it too, because I said it. So who's leading whom?

Peaceful One: Who has the tenacity to remain peaceful no matter what? Who is wise beyond belief and has the power of a universal river of life to back us up? Who has a fleet of Armada ships sailing in all directions and still all end up in Spain?

Joyce: Armadas? Spain? What are you talking about? Well, I can see when I am outdone. Yes, it is best that Higher Mind lead my life and that Conscious Mind follow in cooperation. Wait a minute; did I just say what I think I said? Did I say that you could lead my life, not me?

Peaceful One: Makes sense, since I'm the one making the life for us both. What did you think when you gave up your life to me?

Joyce: It felt like surrender. It wasn't angry. It was kind of sweet, like how two lovers surrender to each other.

Peaceful One: Now you have stopped me in my tracks. Where did you get that? I didn't send that to you. You came up with that yourself.

Joyce: Did I? It just felt like the truth. I was thinking about an experience.

Peaceful One: How grateful you must be for that experience. It was a beautiful one no doubt.

Joyce: Yes, but way too brief. Don't you have experiences and remember the feelings about them?

Peaceful One: Not exactly like you. We come fully prepared to be a support and help and usually take the responsibility of leading a life to a good end, but you supply the experience and that includes emotions. We just get to look and listen.

Joyce: Really! I thought that you had it all and nothing was denied you. I can see that I do have something unique to contribute.

Peaceful One: It's not that it's denied to us; rather it's supplied to us by your living in time and space in human bodies.

Joyce: That is both good and bad. Some of these experiences and emotions feel pretty bad, some very good. It's a mixed bag here on the physical plane.

Peaceful One: Give me one more reason to give you a season of peace between lifetimes. So much more can be said about lifetimes and the differences between the dimensions that we may need more space to discuss it. How about a third book? Are you game for yet more experiences or should I let you take a nap?

Joyce: Are you making fun of me? It's not easy being me. Darn it, now I sound like Kermit the Frog.

Peaceful One: I can take care of you if you just let me be free to be inventive and do not lock us into yet another set of expectations of what is to come that cannot be changed in your mind unless we create WWIII.

Joyce: I can see where this is going. OK, I agree. Let's do a third book. It sounds like the topic will be: Life on the Earth Plane or something like that.

Peaceful One: If you would leave it up to me, I'd say the title should be: Body of Light. Remember that you wrote a fine poem a couple of years ago about The Companions of Peace. They are all Beings of Light. I'd like to use it in my next book.

Joyce: Excuse me! I am the author of this book.

Peaceful One: You and me, babe, and reader make three. See you then.

Joyce: I love you so much.

Peaceful One: Ditto.

Resources

Recommended Websites

PeaceandLight.net

This is our association website, and we offer information on the path to peace, links to other good sites and schedules for classes and conferences. You can purchase a copy of this and future books on Amazon.com in Kindle or softbound form. We will announce future books on the site.

EdgarCayce.org

This is the official website of the Association for Research and Enlightenment, representing the foundation that Edgar Cayce left behind after his death. It houses the library of his readings as well as many other good books and resources. The association has an active lecture and conference schedule, and we teach there often. The center is a beautiful place full of peace, and we highly recommend the meditation garden, library, bookstore and meditation room on the top floor.

HayHouse.com

This is the site for the organization that Louise Hay founded. Her landmark book, *You Can Heal your Life*, has propelled millions on the same path that I am describing here. The organization has conferences, books, an Internet radio program and is generally a great resource for people living the lifestyle of the peaceful and patient.

avisionintoyou.com

This is the site of Jim Herman who is a Medical Intuitive. He has learned from Higher Mind how to help people through asking the Great Oneness to send them healings. He essentially lends his strength of will to that of the petitioner, forming a strong opening for grace. His work is dedicated to the Highest Good, and so thus it is. He gives classes and has individual appointments over the phone or in person to conduct this process.

Peacepiper.net

This is a site created by Phil Crabtree who learned how to channel his Higher Mind. He discovered that in a past life he played music to heal people in ancient Egypt. In this life he is a PhD. in music and has remembered how to channel each person's soul song. He will play your unique healing song and you can record it. It will resonate with you profoundly and bring you much healing. This is just the beginning of the Mystery School Returnees who are finding their life path and special areas of service.

Stephanievanhoose.com

Stephanie learned how to open her channel to her Higher Mind and started doing readings for people. The more she did, the better she got. Now she is developing a radio program called Journey of the Soul for discussion and call-ins on Highest Good topics. I will be appearing on her program often. Check her site for times and channels at www.peakofohio.com.

www.ingramcontent.com/pod-product-compliance
Lightning Source LLC
Chambersburg PA
CBHW071715090426
42738CB00009B/1782